Jesus and the Kingdom of Nobodies

Stories of Compassion

For Faith Sharing

And Homily Preparation

Andre Papineau, SDS

Resource Publications, Inc.
San Jose, California

Reprint Department
Resource Publications, Inc.
160 E. Virginia Street #290
San Jose, CA 95112-5876
1-408-286-8505 (voice)
1-408-287-8748 (fax)

Library of Congress Cataloging-in-Publication Data
Papineau, Andre, 1937–
    Jesus and the kingdom of nobodies : stories of compassion
for faith sharing and homily preparation / Andre Papineau.
        p.   cm.
    Includes bibliographical references.
    ISBN 0-89390-514-3 (pbk.)
    1. Story sermons. 2. Catholic Church—Sermons.
    3. Sermons, American—20th century. 4. Bible. N.T.
    Gospels—Sermons. I. Title
    BV4307.S7 P37 2001
    252—dc21   00-069830

Printed in the United States of America

01 02 03 04 05 | 5 4 3 2 1

Editorial director: Nick Wagner
Production coordinator: Mike Sagara
Copyeditor: Robin Witkin

Contents

Introduction

"Holiness is wholeness." Have you ever heard this expression? If you want to attract the attention of people who are interested in being holy or being whole, then spend an hour or two pointing out how holiness is wholeness. If you want to shine as a complete, healthy, well-adjusted, fully actualized person, we've got news on becoming whole. If you want to please the divine by being holy, we've got news on becoming holy.

Holiness is wholeness. Seems like a happy wedding between two longtime enemies—religion and psychology. It's nice to see that the shrinks and the saints are getting along. There's no need to be suspicious about this relationship, is there? Well, I'd like to think there's no reason to be uneasy, but between you and me, I confess to some misgivings. I'd like to think I'm wrong. After all, the notion that holiness is wholeness has an honorable history in the Bible.

In Leviticus we read "Ye shall be holy, for I the Lord your God am holy." And since God is complete, whole, integral, perfect, it follows that if the folks in Jesus' time were to be holy as God is holy, then they too had to be complete, whole, and integral. This was the way to make God smile and get the community's blessings as well! With such an honorable history, why is there this uneasiness about the holiness-wholeness equation?

Introduction

Could it be that since the injunction to be holy as the Lord God is holy was a basic value, it ended up being the only value among some influential folks in the Jewish community? I'm thinking of the powerful religious elite—aristocrats—people whose opinion mattered very much when it came to identifying where people fit—who was in or out, whole or unwhole, holy or unholy. And if, in a highly stratified society, anyone cared about what others thought, it was important to pay attention to what the elite had to say on maintaining integrity, on losing it, and on getting it back. True, there were some unfortunate people who didn't need to worry about losing their integrity. According to the purity system, they were flawed from day one. Among them were the lame, the blind, the deaf, bastards, eunuchs, and others who were physically impaired. These nobodies are the subjects of this volume of stories.

But uneasy lay the crown on the heads of those who *were* considered whole. They could lose their integrity if they weren't constantly defending their body from contaminants leaving or entering it or if they weren't carefully monitoring contact of any kind with defective persons, places, or things. Too bad for menstruating women or men having seminal emissions or an exchange of bodily fluids with someone socially or physically flawed. Even kissing or hugging or touching the wrong person could be defiling. If they weren't careful, they could become nobodies through their contact with other nobodies.

Eating unclean food alone or with unclean persons was also contaminating. Think how offensive Jesus' sharing Jerusalem rye and lake perch with the crowd in an open space must have seemed to the guardians of wholeness and holiness. Every clean Tom, Dick, and Mary eating with every other unclean Tom, Dick, and Mary in the middle of some godforsaken place! Nothing like blurring the differences between the clean and unclean, between the somebodies and the nobodies! It mattered not a whit to the aristocrats that the folks whom Jesus fed left with full hearts and bellies. That was beside the point for those who zealously pursued the holiness-wholeness equation. It is this matter of eating unclean food that engages Jesus in an argument with the Pharisees in Mark 7:1–17.

The Pharisees objected to Jesus' apparent lack of concern about eating properly prepared food. But his not keeping a kosher kitchen was only the tip of the iceberg. Once more he had challenged what the Pharisees thought was the key to being acceptable to God and to one another—namely, that holiness is wholeness. They were angry that Jesus minimized the importance of safeguarding the body against contact with anything unclean or anyone unclean. But Jesus did not deny what they valued; he simply drew attention to a neglected value. And what was that value? Jesus' comment to his disciples that what comes out of a person's heart is what counts was an amendment to the Pharisees' emphasis on what goes into the body. But Jesus didn't mention the value that motivated him every time he crossed boundaries. And before we consider that value, what needs to be emphasized is that his argument with them was not culture-bound and therefore irrelevant to us.

In a secular society such as ours the struggle many have with being well adjusted and acceptable to others might seem totally unconnected with being holy. After all, being holy does not seem to be a burning issue for swinging singles, Generation X, or anyone looking for a hot date! Yet, the religious fervor with which people seek to be psychologically or physically whole reveals a religious concern about being accepted unconditionally.

For example, folks who become anorexic or bulimic are as religiously concerned about eating kosher food as were the people in Jesus' time. Anorexics are appalled at the thought of eating anything that might make them unclean and thus unacceptable, while bulimics gorge themselves on anything and everything only to cleanse themselves later of what has defiled and made them unacceptable. These disorders signal a larger problem: our culture's misguided priority on what makes a person, especially a woman, whole and acceptable—namely, a shapely, youthful appearance. I won't even mention the cult of the body at the workout centers of worship.

For those of us who aren't too concerned about eating habits, may I suggest that our concern about bodily integrity and purity shows up in our purchase of those guardians of the bodies' portals we call deodorant, scented soap, perfume, cologne, shaving lotion, and toothpaste. And the Jewish elite thought they had the corner on purity.

But what I have said about purity concerns in our culture is equally present in the church as we reflect about who's in or out, whole or unwhole, and the consequences for the folks who suffer contamination. Priests who marry—*unclean!* People who divorce, remarry, and want to share in the Eucharist—*unclean!* When Ted Kennedy shared communion at his mother's funeral liturgy, tongues were wagging until someone breathed a sigh of relief that his first marriage had been annulled. Thank God, he was really clean and whole after all! And while we're on the Kennedys, recall Jackie Kennedy Onassis' funeral—tongues were wagging then. Hadn't she been living in an unclean relationship? How could she be buried from the church? Unclean! And, what's this world coming to, women who contemplate ordination! The very thought of it! Unclean! Or Christians crossing denominational boundaries to share the Eucharist, uniting themselves with Jesus, the boundary crosser. Unclean!

Introduction

"Good God!" we think. "What's going to happen to us? How can we retain our integrity? This blurring of who's in and who's out is going to create an identity problem. We won't know who we are anymore! What will happen to wholeness? To holiness? To what makes us acceptable or unacceptable to others and to God?" Who said the purity system was a thing of the past?

Well, while being pure or whole is a component of our identity, there is another value that enters into the picture. Jesus reached out to all flawed persons, to the nobodies he came across. What motivated him to do so was *compassion*, the value that includes rather than excludes, that shows no partiality. In compassion Jesus reverses and turns upside-down the idea that some folks are in and some are out. The *lowly* shall be raised up and the mighty shall be humbled; the first shall be last and the last first. Jesus' preference for the lowly, the unclean, is his preference for the nobodies in his society. For Jesus, God's holiness is as much a matter of compassion as it is of wholeness.

Holiness is wholeness. Yes, I have reservations about elevating this slogan to a place of eminence if it excludes the value of compassion that Jesus embodied time and again as he crossed boundaries and reached out to make the nobodies into somebodies.

Holiness is wholeness. If we preached this with the same single-minded devotion that the Jewish elite did when Jesus was crossing boundaries, we would have had to exclude him from our guest list as we met him at the door and cried "Unclean!"

I am indebted to Dominic Crossan for the expression "Jesus and the Kingdom of Nobodies" in his book, *Jesus: A Revolutionary Biography*. It is a fitting way of describing the people Jesus sought to people the kingdom of God. And it is these people's stories I have written.

How to Use These Stories

Parish leaders, or homilists, or small faith-sharing groups, or RCIA groups, or high school teenagers will find the stories and the reflections following the stories helpful in deepening their appreciation of Jesus' compassion for those who are treated as nobodies. They will be challenged to reach out to the nobodies in their midst.

Faith-sharing groups can be challenged to see beyond limited horizons of who God is and what God expects of them. Even with the best of intentions, small groups can become preoccupied with their own needs and neglect the needs of the larger church community, which envisions God as reaching out to all God's children.

Homilists may be stimulated to use the stories as their homilies. The reflections can serve as the direction(s) in which the homilist hopes to move the congregation in presenting the story. Of course, the homilist is free to adapt the stories and present them as he or she feels suits the occasion. Many of the stories can be delivered by two or three persons during the liturgy on special occasions.

Older high school students can relate to these stories because they are about insiders or cliques rejecting those who appear odd or different from the group for any number of reasons (e.g., physical disability, different moral standards, etc.). It would be helpful for teachers or catechists to guide discussions through the use of the reflections, especially if these reflections lead the teenagers to reflect on their own concerns about being rejected. Teens fear being outsiders because the consequences (e.g., loneliness, loss of self-esteem, etc.) are so frightening and even destructive, as evidenced in the tragedies at Columbine High School in Colorado.

What is often overlooked in using stories is the possibility of presenting an *evening of storytelling* by older teenagers for an audience or church congregation. Teenagers who are talented storytellers or show potential can be invited to participate by choosing stories that are humorous or serious. During the course of the evening, one person can present a story having little or no dialogue, and then two or three can present a story that has enough dialogue for several persons. One of the teenagers can act as a narrator for the evening by providing a thematic context, such as how Jesus reaches out to the nobodies, and then leading into the various storytellers and their stories with the different ways in which Jesus embraces the physically disabled, the morally bankrupt, the foreigners. Storytelling is a very effective way of communicating the Gospel message to people who might be disinclined to listen to lectures on spiritual themes but are open to listening to stories.

These stories can be used in *catechumenate* groups to illustrate that being a Christian is certainly a call to holiness but that the zeal to be holy can be excessive if it isn't accompanied by compassion. Becoming Christian means among other things being inclusive and universal in one's concerns. The stories of Jesus' outreach to the alienated and foreigners can be used to emphasize the church as a transnational community, a global community whose interests ought to be the well-being of all Christians.

Persons preparing others for *confirmation* will find many of these stories helpful since they frequently present situations in which the characters show courage and determination to do the right thing in spite of seemingly insurmountable obstacles. Again the reflections are helpful in leading

individuals to reflect on whether they are willing to follow
through on their own convictions and what being confirmed
entails.

If the stories are used with children, it should be obvious
from reading them that not all are suited for children. And
whenever a story is used, the teacher will need to adapt it to
the children's ability to understand the story.

Finally, it seems that however the different groups or
individuals use the stories, some groups might find it helpful
to begin by reading the entire Gospel passage on which the
story is based since many persons might not be familiar with
it. The value of reading the Gospel passage is enhanced when
individuals are stimulated to share their own insights. The
stories serve as a catalyst for these insights to occur.

However these stories are used, they are about the nobodies
of the world who have been welcomed and embraced by Jesus,
who preached about the reign of God and the kingdom of
nobodies.

1. How Hark Became The Herald

In that region there were shepherds living in the
fields, keeping watch over their flock by night. Then
an angel of the Lord stood before them, and the glory
of the Lord shone around them, and they were terri-
fied. But the angel said to them, "Do not be afraid; for
see—I am bringing you good news of great joy for all
the people: to you is born this day in the city of David
a Savior, who is the Messiah, the Lord. This will be a
sign for you: you will find a child wrapped in bands of
cloth and lying in a manger." And suddenly there was
with the angel a multitude of the heavenly host,
praising God and saying,
   "Glory to God in the highest heaven,
   and on earth peace among those whom he favors!"
   (Luke 2:8–15)

Ever since Hark was a little angel he was a squawker—not
exactly what you'd expect from an angel. When he was
born at Holy Angels Hospital on Cloud Nine Drive, the
medical squadron of angels and angelettes couldn't believe
their ears. Because they had never heard a baby with such a
strong set of lungs, they initially thought an off-duty angel
had gone berserk on a trumpet—that is, until they flew past
the nursery and heard Hark exercising his vocal cords.

1. How Hark Became the Herald

Frantically, they flew in every direction seeking ways to turn down Hark's volume. Nobody was sure what to do. Finally, they decided to wing it and try their best to quiet him. But no matter what they did—cradle him gently in their wings, give him an extra-cushy cloud to lie on or extra time to feather down next to his mother—they failed. "Hark! Shhh! Shhh! Shhh!" they whispered over and over. Hark's mother was a little annoyed when the nurses occasionally taped his mouth shut so the other little angels could get some shut-eye.

Then an unusual number of saints began showing up at Holy Angels. Hearing the brassy tones booming through the hospital walls, they thought it was their cue to come marching in! Oh when the saints go marching in!

You can imagine how relieved the staff was when it was time for Hark's family to gather him up and wing their way home. Hark's departure was good news for the hospital staff, but it was something else again for his neighbors. They had no idea what was in store for them. All the other little angels had acted as little angels were expected to act—like little angels, of course! But because Hark sounded like a trumpet at full blast he didn't seem to be a little angel at all. His neighbors were left with nothing but a wing and a prayer that they'd get some divine rest.

Nowhere in the heavenly realm were the words "Shhh! Shhh! Shhh!" heard so often. Placing a finger to their lips, the angels whispered, "Hark! Shhh! Shhh! Shhh!" whenever they saw or heard him. Even when he wasn't around, they'd whisper "Shhh! Shhh! Shhh!" For example, they'd sit down for dinner, take a bite of pasta (angel hair, of course), go "Shhh! Shhh! Shhh!", sip a glass of red wine, then another "Shhh! Shhh! Shhh!", back to the pasta, and so on. Obviously this didn't make for exciting table talk!

1. How Hark Became the Herald

At first Hark thought his full name was "Hark! Shhh! Shhh! Shhh!" You see, he was just too young to understand what the other angels were asking of him. Besides, he often got so loud that he couldn't hear them anyway. What bothered Hark's family and friends didn't affect him until he was about two years old. Then he began to catch on that he was the reason the angels around him were wringing their wings. So when Hark flapped his wings in the tub and made all kinds of noise, his mom shook her head and warned, "Hark! Shhh! Shhh! Shhh! Pipe down! You're too loud! Be a good little angel. Fold your hands and stop flapping your wings. You'll wear them out!"

Hark was beginning to get the message. As he grew older, Hark loved to yodel in the shower or sing in the rain, causing tremors throughout the heavens. Angels slipped off clouds and even lost their halos. Hark's mom and dad panicked! "Hark! Shhh! Shhh! Shhh! You're becoming a nuisance. Keep this up and there'll be no more angel food cake for you! Just devil's food cake! Do you hear?" "Ohhh," Hark groaned. Devil's food cake! The thought of horns and a long tail instead of wings and a halo scared him as nothing else had. Until he got to school.

There his teachers warned him, "Hark! Shhh! Shhh! Shhh! We're afraid of all hell breaking loose every time you open your mouth. And that's the last thing we need to happen here, in heaven of all places! Keep it up, and we'll see to it that you get your wings clipped!"

Hark was so sad. The other angels thought that he was a real pain. He wondered, "What good am I if all I have is a big mouth with a trumpet for a voice that makes all the other angels nervous. All I ever hear is 'Hark! Shhh! Shhh! Shhh! Keep quiet! Pipe down!' What kind of a future do I have?" Tears rolled down his cheeks as he buried his head in his wings. "Why did I end up with this big mouth?" He didn't have to wait long to find out.

The next day a mighty big angel flew in to see Hark. Hark knew immediately this was no ordinary angel. He had the wingspan of a 747—and then some! The angel smiled and said, "Hello Hark. I'm the Archangel Michael, but you can call me Mike. I've come from headquarters. God would like to see you."

Hark's eyes widened as he trumpeted, "GOD WANTS TO SEE ME!"

"Hark! Shhh! Shhh! Shhh! Not so loud. Yeah! The boss has something important to tell you. So spread your wings and follow me."

Hark began to worry. Since everyone else was upset with him, he figured word had gotten out to God and now God was about to lecture him or—even worse— punish him. As these thoughts raced through Hark's mind, his wings sagged a bit, but he finally got them flapping at full speed as he trailed Mike to God's house. He had never been to the boss's place before. So he was mightily impressed when he landed safely on the angels' landing pad in front of the boss's residence. Something big was ready to happen. There were angels and angelettes flying to and fro. An air of excitement filled the house. In one of the rooms Hark noticed a whole choir of angels rehearsing for some special occasion. Mike led Hark into God's outer office. As Hark sat there, he wondered what his fate might be. Maybe he'd be working in a soundproof room forever! Or sent to Angels Monastery where the angels never talked and just communicated by flapping their wings in a kind of Morse code.

1. How Hark Became the Herald

Finally, an angel dressed in white edged in blinking lights entered the room and told him God was ready to see him. No sooner had Hark entered the big office than a huge man marched over to Hark, placed his arm around Hark's shoulder, smiled broadly, and cried in a booming voice, "Hi Hark! I'm God, in case you didn't know! You're just the angel I've been looking for. They tell me you've got the biggest, brassiest voice in the heavens. Terrific!"

Hark was dumbfounded. "Terrific!" the boss boomed again—louder than Hark had ever boomed. He sounded like a tuba with the New York Philharmonic. Hark was delirious with joy. All along he had thought there was something wrong with him. But now he knew he was in good company. Not even one of the newer saints to arrive, Doc Severinson, could produce sounds like God! God continued. "And I've got just the right job for you, Hark! I need an angel like you—we call them heralds—to let the people on Earth know that we've got fantastic news for them. My son is going to be born among them. Hark, do you think you could be my chief herald? Do you think you could pull it off? You gotta be loud! You gotta be brassy! You gotta sing your lungs out! Can you spread your wings and be my herald?"

Hark was overwhelmed. The boss wanted him to do what nobody else had ever asked him to do—to be loud and brassy in the heavens and on Earth! At that minute Hark felt he could spread his wings and do a thousand things he had never done before. "Yes! Yes! I can do it!" Hark boomed.

"Good! Good!" the boss bellowed. "Then it's on your way. We've got a backup choir for you in the next room and we'll throw in a few harpists for good measure. I'm not crazy about harps but people expect them. It goes with being an angel! But it's up to you to lead the way and bring the news. You've got a great gift! And don't let anyone tell you otherwise," the boss winked as he embraced Hark and escorted him to the door.

Hark was ecstatic as he flew down the corridors and out of God's house. The choir that had been rehearsing gathered in back of Hark and began practicing the good news they would soon proclaim, "Glory, glory, glory! Peace on earth, good will to all!" They also decided to throw in a song in honor of their leader, Hark. And of course we know the song.

Once Hark and the choir descended through the clouds to Earth, Hark trumpeted the message of his life to shepherds in a field. Finally, he knew why he had been born with the loudest, brassiest voice in the heavens.

Reflection

How can a handicap become a gift? Hark has a voice that annoys everyone who hears it. It's loud and brassy! As with many of the other characters in the following stories, Hark doesn't fit in. Admittedly, it is a different community, the community of angels! He doesn't fit because he deviates from what is normal for angels; he doesn't have a sweet, soft voice.

However, God delights in Hark's voice, finding it appealing and useful. God chooses Hark to carry out a job that only Hark seems able to do. Hark realizes that his voice, which had annoyed so many angels, is actually a great gift. And why? Because of God's affirmation of that gift.

Even though this story is about an angel, it could easily be the story of many boys and girls whose talents at first seem to be a handicap rather than a blessing. Think of comics W. C. Fields and Jimmy Durante. They weren't gifted with good looks, but they were able to use their looks to become successful screen and stage stars. Or how about actors

1. How Hark Became the Herald

Christopher Reeves and Michael Fox? Reeves suffered a paralyzing injury when he fell from a horse and Fox discovered he has a chronic, debilitating disease. Their lights have shone in new ways since Reeves became a spokesperson on behalf of spinal cord injuries and Fox on behalf of persons with Parkinson's disease.

Our ability to see our gifts as gifts depends on our parents and friends. Their admiration serves as a catalyst in recognizing that we have something valuable to offer others. It is sad is when gifts go unrecognized and unused.

Hark's gift made him a nuisance among the other angels. But his call from God demonstrated that what is unacceptable in some eyes is acceptable in others. And in the final analysis, it is how we appear in God's eyes that counts.

2. Where the Power Is

When they had heard the king, they set out; and
there, ahead of them, went the star that they had
seen at its rising, until it stopped over the place
where the child was. When they saw that the star had
stopped, they were overwhelmed with joy. On entering the house, they saw the child with Mary his
mother; and they knelt down and paid him homage.
(Matthew 2:9–11)

The two kings had never met until they crossed each
other's path, but they quickly recognized each other as
kings. Both were dressed in royal robes that partially
concealed body armor so heavy that even their camels seemed
relieved when they dismounted. And servants assisted them
lest they trip over the long trains on their robes.

Treated as powerful monarchs by their subjects, each
waited for the other to extend a greeting. Eyeing one another
suspiciously, they both finally managed a cautious hello. But
what do kings anxious to assert power do next? Blurt out
their credentials, of course!

"I am His Majesty King Boris the Bald, son of Boris the
Balder, from the land—"

King Toot interrupted, "And I am His Majestic Majesty King Toot, son of Toot the Tooter, from the powerful land—"

"Majestic Majesty?" King Boris snorted. "Well, as I was saying, I am from a feared country where our citizens bear mighty arms and learn frightening grunts and growls to threaten strangers who—"

King Toot quickly upped the ante. "In my country we teach our citizens not only to grunt and growl but to warn our enemy by tooting fearsome body sounds! Think on that one for a minute!" he added gravely. King Boris quickly backed up a couple of steps and covered his nose with a royal hanky lest King Toot harbor any nasty ideas about him!

Mistaking King Boris's move as a sign of weakness, King Toot relaxed and asked, "Where are you traveling?"

Mistaking King Toot's friendliness as a sign of weakness, King Boris smiled and answered, "My starstruck astrologer told me that a powerful king in a distant land has a powerful message for me if I'd follow a special star leading me to this king. Accompanying me are my men, Boris's Bouncing Bangers." Pointing to them, Boris said, "They are the most muscular, meanest looking subjects in my realm. I have had them fitted in heavy armor, armed with heavy-duty spears, and loaded with some of these same spears for the powerful king."

King Toot could hardly contain himself. "I too have gotten word from my starstruck astrologer that a powerful king has a powerful message for me! And since my astrologer has graduated with honors from Tooterville U, I have complete confidence in him. He also directed me to follow a star to the powerful king." No slouch when it came to weapons, he added,

"I have armed my men in heavy armor as well. And they wear gas masks!"

Of course this was a thinly veiled way of informing King Boris that no matter how fearsome the body noises got from Boris's Bouncing Bangers, King Toot was prepared. Beads of perspiration formed on Boris the Bald's pate as Toot added that his men were equipped with state-of-the-art spears. Toot bared his teeth and growled, "My spears can be converted into giant peashooters. Then my men can spit leaden balls through them and destroy armies as powerful as your Bouncing Bangers." Pointing proudly to his men, King Toot added, "My men are twice the size of the renowned giant, Arble Schwarzenbanger, and they are known far and wide as the Towering Toots!"

Having described how powerful they were, the kings agreed their meeting one another was hardly a coincidence since they were following the same star to the same powerful king. So they decided to journey together in the interest of power.

What neither had anticipated was how far they'd have to travel to reach the powerful king. As each day passed on the long trek through the hot desert, the kings in their heavy robes felt more and more burdened while their soldiers encased in heavy armor neared exhaustion.

Fortunately, at an oasis, the kings met a party of men who were journeying in the same direction. From the men's appearance, it was obvious that they had no royal connections. They were dressed simply and were unarmed, much to the surprise of the kings. King Toot wondered how anyone journeying through the desert could survive without weapons. King Boris heartily agreed.

2. Where the Power Is

Their spokesperson never mentioned anything about belonging to a powerful kingdom nor did he chat about the latest hi-tech weaponry or react to King Toot's description of his state-of-the-art spears. This disturbed the kings. What could they discuss with this young man if not power? But they changed their minds when he said, "I am also following a star that a wise man told me would lead me to a king with a powerful message." Yet he made no mention of a powerful king, just a king with a powerful message.

Shaking their heads, King Toot and King Boris thought this man probably hadn't gotten the message straight. Anyone who has a powerful message must also be a powerful king. How could you have one without the other? But they didn't think it wise to argue. Instead, they drew the young man aside and asked if he and his friends would help them. As an incentive the kings promised to arm the young man and his friends with weapons galore.

After consulting his friends the young man told the kings, "We will help you provided you leave behind all the weapons you've offered us in exchange for our help." King Toot and King Boris were dumbfounded! "Sir, do you know what you're saying?" King Toot asked. "How can you refuse to arm yourselves with state-of-the-art weapons, especially the peashooters?"

"Either you accept our offer or the deal is off," the young man insisted. Noting how serious the man was and aware they couldn't continue the journey without him, they reluctantly agreed. Sadly they waved good-bye to the weapons left in the desert sand and resumed their journey.

After traveling three more days, they reached another oasis. The young man drew the kings aside. "You're going to have to leave behind the rest of your weapons," he said.

2. Where the Power Is

"What?" the kings gasped. "Why?" they demanded.

The young man calmly explained, "We still have a long way to go. We'll never arrive at our destination unless we dump these heavy weapons here. If you decide you want to bring them with you, then we'll no longer be able to accompany you."

Again the kings objected strenuously. Boris balked and Toot twitted. "What kind of power can we have if we wave good-bye to our hi-tech giant peashooters? It's not fair! It's not right!" Yet while they weren't ready to admit it, they had felt a sense of relief when they had discarded the weapons at the first oasis. Certain that they had convinced each other how upset they were over the young man's conditions, they mumbled, "OK! OK! If that's what you want!" So they shed a few tears as they dumped their heavy weapons in the sand and continued on their journey.

A strange thing began to happen. The kings began to feel lighthearted and carefree. They talked less about power. They relaxed. Even the Towering Toots and the Bouncing Bangers were friendlier. One by one the Towering Toots soon dropped their gas masks on the desert floor.

A few days later the young man spoke to the kings yet again. "We can't go on with you unless you leave behind your armor and your royal robes. We have enough light clothes that you can wear. They're simple but comfortable."

The kings were indignant. "We'll look like everybody else without our purple boxer shorts, robes and armor," King Toot complained.

21

"And what will the powerful king say when he sees us dressed like … well, like you?" King Boris added. "Surely he'll dismiss us as weak kings unfit to rule. He'll turn us away."

But the young man was unyielding.

The kings pouted and nearly told the young man he could hit the dust. Yet in their hearts they knew he had actually brought them closer together. They talked freely about their families and friends. They even admitted how they secretly admired some of their subjects who courageously refused to grunt and growl toward strangers. They talked less and less about power.

So they gave in to the young man's request. Stripping themselves of their regal clothes right down to their underwear, they commanded their troops to do the same. In an instant the Towering Toots and the Bouncing Bangers were shouting alleluias as they too stripped to their underwear and joyfully danced in a circle. Then the kings ordered them to take whatever food they needed and continue on the journey.

No sooner had they abandoned all trappings of power than the star they had been following led them to a small cave in the side of a hill. Why had the star stopped here? they wondered. Their astrologers had said it would lead them to a powerful king with a powerful message. But what powerful king would live in a cave on the side of the hill? The young man reminded them that his wise counselor had said the journey would lead them not to a powerful king but to a king with a powerful message. The two kings shrugged their shoulders. They didn't know what to think.

The three men entered the cave. All they saw was a young couple with a small child lying in a manger surrounded by a few sheep. Scratching their heads, the kings introduced themselves. Then King Toot whispered to King Boris, "If this is a king, why isn't he dressed like one?"

King Boris agreed, "If this infant has a powerful message, how can he talk about it?"

As they wondered about these things, the mother of the infant graciously thanked them for coming. She said she wished she had a meal fit for the three kings but all she could give them was some porridge she had made. The kings looked at each other. "Three kings?" they muttered. Where did she get the idea there were three kings? As far as they knew they were the only kings who had entered the cave. The only other person accompanying them was the young man. They had introduced themselves as kings but the young man had remained silent.

The young woman laughed. "Of course you're all kings," she insisted. The young man smiled but still said nothing. She added cryptically, "Real kings don't need to talk about what makes them a king or where their power is, do they?"

As she spoke, the two kings' eyes widened as they looked at the young man. What they had learned from him on the journey was that all their talk about power and the trappings of power meant little compared with the joy they had experienced as they rid themselves of their powerful weapons in the desert. Surely, the kings thought, this young man was the kind of king she was talking about. And this naked child, so defenseless, was both a king and a powerful message. In this child they discovered that you don't need to be powerfully armed to have a powerful message. Thereupon the three kings graciously thanked mother and father, reverenced the baby, and left the cave. They had discovered where real power is.

Reflection

Where is the power? A series of wars this past century left millions dead. And we continue to use our power to oppress and victimize others as well as to defend ourselves. We also witness abuses of power in our governing bodies when lobbyists representing different interest groups wine and dine officials. Abuses of power exist in the church when ecclesiastical authorities silence laypersons, priests, and nuns because they have spoken out on an issue regarded as sacrosanct by these authorities. We read of the abuses of parental power in which parents sexually or emotionally abuse their children. Positions of leadership bring with them the temptation to abuse power. And where has the destructive use of power gotten us?

The kings in this story flex their muscles and bare their teeth at each other until they gradually discover, through the third king, that they can appreciate each other's presence by abandoning the trappings of power. As they approach the manger, they realize that genuine community comes into being when they abandon their defensive posturing.

The king they meet in Jesus mirrors who they are already becoming—individuals whose power lies not in powerful armies, arms, or royal insignia but in a personal presence through which they recognize and appreciate their common humanity. The king they meet is powerless, but his message is powerful. It is a message we need to hear in our own time as the abuses of power continue.

3. What's in a Name?

Her husband Joseph, being a righteous man and un-willing to expose her to public disgrace, planned to dismiss her quietly. But just when he had resolved to do this, an angel of the Lord appeared to him in a dream and said, "Joseph, son of David, do not be afraid to take Mary as your wife, for the child con-ceived in her is from the Holy Spirit. She will bear a son, and you are to name him Jesus, for he will save his people from their sins." All this took place to fulfill what had been spoken by the Lord through the prophet:

"Look, the virgin shall conceive and bear a son,
and they shall name him Emmanuel,"
which means, "God is with us." (Matthew 1:19–23)

He had read or heard somewhere that a person's destiny was related to his or her name. He was aware of only a few people whose names seemed linked to their professions. Dr. Foot had treated the calluses on his dad's feet. And Mrs. Rose ran a florist shop next to the apartment building where he lived. And how could he forget old Mr. Cleaver, the butcher in the meat market down the block. He chuckled as he recalled hearing his dad talk about his old friend Henry Hogg who ran a pig farm outside the city. Then he winced. "Ferris Finke," he muttered. "Yeah, Ferris Finke. Destiny? What destiny?" he wondered. If he had been able to choose a name, he certainly wouldn't have chosen Ferris Finke. And of all times to be saddled with his name, Ferris thought this was the worst.

Ferris was a tenth-grade student at a large high school in the South Bronx. In and out of class, he was reminded how humiliating it was to be called Ferris Finke.

"Hey, how's our little fink doing today?" he'd hear as he walked through the school corridors on his way to class. Or, "Finke's a ferrie! Finke's a ferrie! Finke's a ferrie" as he'd turn his back to open a door. And it wasn't unusual to find notes with the same thing scribbled on them plastered onto his locker. Sometimes as soon as he'd leave school, the school bullies would elbow him and whisper, "Are you Ferrie Finke or Finke Ferrie?" Then they'd imitate the way he spoke and walked.

Ferris was frail looking, lisped slightly, and had certain effeminate mannerisms. So the bullies had an easy target as they mimicked his gestures and gait while they made fun of his name. Often he came home with a bloody nose and torn clothing. No wonder he dreaded going to school.

Although the bullying was bad, the teachers were difficult as well. They unintentionally made him the butt of more jokes when they called his name in class. The beginning of each school year was especially difficult. His new teachers always embarrassed him as they tried to get his name straight. Because his last name was spelled F-i-n-k-e, many teachers called loudly and clearly on the first class day, "Ferris, do you pronounce it Fink or Finkie? I know someone whose name is Finke without the e." But it didn't end there. Then they'd start on his first name.

"Ferris? Where does that name come from? Were you named after the person who invented the Ferris Wheel?" He could have told them that his parents gave him the name simply because they loved how it sounded. They had no other reason. No one else in the family had been named Ferris. His parents didn't know anyone with the name. His mother loved his name so much that when he was down the block playing she'd belt out his name as if she were hawking newspapers on a street corner. Mealtime would roll around and it would be, "Ferrissss! Come and get it! All the food that's fit to eat! Ferrisss! Ferrisss!" Ferris would run home as fast as he could just to get his mother to quiet down.

As for the name Finke—his whole family was stuck with that one! No choice there. Over the years, he'd figured out how to minimize some of the embarrassment. For example, he decided not to discuss how he got his name with his teachers; that simply provoked more snickers from his classmates. He spoke as little as possible and never sat in the back of the room if he had a choice. Whenever possible, Ferris sat in the front seat near the door, where he could whisper to his teachers. That had worked until this year. Now he had Miss Bellows, who was hard of hearing. Unless a name was repeated three times she didn't hear it. And evidently she thought her students had the same problem because she'd repeat everything three times.

"Miss Bellows, my name is Ferris Finke, Ferris Finke, Ferris Finke!"

"Oh, how nice! It's Ferris Finke, Ferris Finke, Ferris Finke!"

Defeated, Ferris slumped in his chair and muttered, "Escape, escape, escape!"

No wonder Ferris found small comfort in discovering that a name could actually reveal something about its bearer. If this were true he dreaded his future. He was so preoccupied as he boarded the bus one cold, wintry day just before Christmas that he hardly noticed the all-too-familiar taunts coming from the back of the bus. Once he did, he felt his stomach tighten. What now? Glancing back he saw the familiar faces making fun of an elderly man wrapped in an old, tattered coat. The man looked frightened and cold. Ferris sat down. No need to get in the middle of someone else's mess. He had problems of his own. But as the taunts continued, Ferris began to feel uneasy. He knew how the old man felt—under attack by those bullies! But he didn't move.

Then a strange thing happened. He heard a faint voice calling, "Ferris Finke, help that man! Ferris Finke, help that man!" The voice grew louder, more persistent! "Ferris, you've got to help that man!" Ferris sighed. Try as he might he couldn't ignore that voice.

He rose slowly to his feet, checking to see if he had a handkerchief since he needed one whenever the bullies bloodied his nose. Yes, he had one. This would probably be the only thing he had to be grateful for on this trip. Taking a deep breath, Ferris walked to where the old man was huddled against the window. Removing his own coat, he gently draped it around the old man's shoulders. A few of those who had been making fun of the old man continued jeering, but the other passengers were silent.

Ferris sat next to the old man and introduced himself. As he spoke something in the tone of his voice was different from the other times he had introduced himself. He almost sounded proud, proud to be Ferris. It surprised him. "Yup, I'm Ferris Finke!" Spinning around he looked directly at the bullies and cried, "I'm Ferris Finke! Get it?"

The old man commented, "That's a mighty nice name. My name's Emmanuel. But you can call me Manny."

"Emmanuel? Hmmm, Emmanuel!" Ferris paused. He wondered if that name meant anything. "Well, Manny, I'll help you home. I think you need the coat more than I do." When they reached the next bus stop, Ferris helped the old man to his feet and guided him to the front of the bus. The bus driver smiled at Ferris as he opened the door and, in a voice that could be heard throughout the bus, said, "Ferris, I'm proud of you!" A loud round of applause and a cry of "Right on, Ferris!" echoed throughout the bus.

Ferris Finke had discovered the meaning of his name.

Reflection

Teenagers like Ferris attend all of our schools. They are the "oddballs," the "weirdos," the objects of others' taunts, and the targets of bullies. Much has been written about teenagers like Ferris ever since the tragedy at Columbine High School in Littleton, Colorado.

What is admirable about Ferris is that he is a survivor. He thinks of ways he can protect himself from the bullies. And even though he often fails, he doesn't give up. Every day he goes back to the school where he is a loner.

Unlike some teenagers who seek revenge for the treatment they receive, Ferris's unhappy experiences help him to find compassion for another victim. In this experience Ferris finds his voice and the meaning of his name. A nobody becomes a somebody in helping another nobody.

This is the path Jesus followed. He was a peasant, a nobody. He understood what it meant to be a nobody and made it his mission to reach out to others to proclaim that in God's kingdom all nobodies are somebodies.

4. Surprise!

But wanting to justify himself, he asked Jesus, "And who is my neighbor?" Jesus replied, "A man was going down from Jerusalem to Jericho, and fell into the hands of robbers, who stripped him, beat him, and went away, leaving him half dead. (Luke 10:29–30)

Fags," Clem sneered as he trotted down the highway to his pickup truck. "They're all a bunch of fairies, and we've given them what they deserve—a bashing on their own turf!"

Earlier that evening, Clem and four buddies had waited in the bushes outside a gay bar until around midnight, when three men came out. As the men walked past the bushes, Clem whispered, "Let's get 'em!" Without any warning they overpowered the men, dragging them to a nearby patch of woods. There they kicked, punched, and pummeled them until they collapsed. Afterward, Clem and the others celebrated at a small house not too far from the bar. Around 2 A.M. they decided to head for home.

"A good night's work," Clem thought as he reached his truck. "That oughtta teach them a lesson that there's no room for dirt around here." Absorbed in his thoughts, he failed to notice two figures huddled near the rear of the truck. No

4. Surprise!

sooner had Clem unlocked the door than he was jumped from behind, knocked to the ground, and beaten senseless.

"Now you know what it feels like," one man cried. The other knelt and looked into Clem's face.

"Oh, no," Clem moaned as he recognized one of the men he and his friends had attacked hours earlier.

"How'd you like to have a little fun?" the other man sneered, ripping off Clem's clothing.

"No, no," Clem pleaded. Clem thought he knew what these men were up to, and that's exactly what they wanted him to think.

"Don't worry!" they laughed. "You're not worth it!" Then they spit on him and walked away, leaving him naked.

There was little traffic that early in the morning, and Clem lay there for about thirty minutes before a Cadillac drove by. At first, the driver didn't seem to notice Clem sprawled out next to his truck. But the car hadn't gone more than a couple hundred feet, when it stopped and backed up. The driver slowly opened the door, placing one foot on the pavement as if he couldn't decide what to do. He was wearing a black suit and a white clerical collar. He mumbled something about gays and their lifestyle as he glanced up the road toward the gay bar. Looking back at Clem, he shook his head and said to himself, "See what comes of it!" Glancing at his watch he quickly withdrew his foot from the pavement, closed the door, rolled the window down, and weakly apologized, "Sorry I can't help. Gotta sick call down the road! Somebody will come along." As he rolled up the window he offered a few words of advice. "Maybe you oughtta think about changing your lifestyle, Buster!" Then he was off to a sick call—or so he said.

About another half hour passed before a Pontiac rolled by.
Bumper stickers were plastered everywhere on the back of
the car. "Jesus loves you more than you know." "Jesus is my
co-pilot." "Jesus is my personal Lord and Savior." This driver
also stopped about a hundred feet down the road, and then
reversed and stopped near Clem's truck. He rolled down the
window and shook his head. Then looking in his rear-view
mirror, he spotted the bar up the road. Sticking his head out
the window and shaking his finger at Clem, he began, "Yeah!
We pray for you fellows. Been getting drunk at your favorite
bar, haven't you? Don't you fellas know the wages of sin is
death? When are you gonna learn where all this leads—to hell
of course! You want sympathy? You'll get sympathy all
right—when you straighten out your life! And when you do, if
you do, come and see me. My name's Deacon Felwall." Having
delivered his lifesaving sermon, the good deacon hurled his
plastic-coated calling card out the window and it landed on
Clem's head. Then he rolled up the window, started the car,
and sped away.

A half hour passed and another car came down the
highway. But this car was moving very slowly and weaving
slightly, occasionally crossing into the other lane. The car
stopped alongside Clem. It must have taken at least five
minutes for the driver to slowly open the door and gingerly
step out. His clothes were disheveled, his forehead and nose
were caked with dried blood, and his eyes were almost
swollen closed. As he limped toward Clem, he held one hand
on his hip as if it hurt.

Staring down at Clem for a minute, he winced as he knelt
to get a closer look. "Oh no! No way!" he moaned. Slowly
rising to his feet, he limped to his car. He didn't look back at
Clem. He climbed painfully back into his car, shut the door,
put his head on the steering wheel, and sobbed. After a few
minutes, he turned on the ignition and began driving down

the highway. About a mile down the road, he slowed and stopped. "I can't leave him there. I just can't," he said as he banged his fist repeatedly on the steering wheel. Turning the car around, he headed back to where Clem lay. Once more he limped over to Clem's body. "Fag, am I? Now we both know what it's like to be beaten half to death. I'd like to say the hell with you! But I can't. I can't wish this on anybody else!"

By now Clem was regaining consciousness. Opening his eyes he tried to focus on the person looking down at him. The face looked vaguely familiar but Clem couldn't place it. "Help me," he whispered.

"Yeah! Yeah!" the man answered. "I don't want to help you, but who else is gonna stop in the middle of the night. Some priest maybe. But I wouldn't count on it!" Clem began to shake violently. The man limped back to his car and hauled out an old beach blanket he had purchased years earlier at a Gay Pride Fest. There were faded slogans all over the blanket: "Gay is great!" "I'm gay and proud of it!" "Gay rights for all!" The man grinned as he draped the blanket over Clem's shoulders and gently lifted him to his feet. Leaning against each other they limped back to the car.

Once inside the car the man drove back to the gay bar. "This guy is gonna make a remarkably fast recovery once he finds out where he is," he thought. When they entered the bar there were still a few patrons sitting around. They were startled when they saw the man helping Clem through the door. "Hey, Ralph," the man called to the bartender, "this guy's been through the mill. So have I, but I'm in better shape than he is. More gay bashing tonight! I found him by the side of the road. I think some of those rednecks got to him."

"That's tough! Know his name? Face isn't familiar. Just the blanket!"

"I dunno." The man knew he couldn't tell Ralph who this guy was.

"OK, Matt. Let's put him on the cot in the back room for a day."

"Great! I'll come around later. If he needs a doctor, I'll get one. By the way, maybe it would help if you'd play some Streisand records. Bet he'd love to hear her sing 'People.'"

"Sure."

"And one more thing," Matt added. "Tell him I'll talk with him about what happened tonight. I'm sure he'll be surprised."

Reflection

Often when people share their Good Samaritan stories, they portray the Samaritan as good because he or she helps someone who is needy. But the Samaritan in Jesus' parable was an enemy of the Jew he saved. He was ethnically and religiously different. Jews and Samaritans hated one another with the same intensity as Jews and Palestinians or Serbs and Kosovar Albanians. That is what makes the story interesting. If the Jew knew a Samaritan was helping him he might have preferred dying since he became unclean by the Samaritan's touch. Even the oil and the wine the Samaritan gave to the Jew were unclean because they weren't kosher. If we understand this enmity, we can better appreciate this story.

A gay-bashing redneck is helped by one of the gays beaten up by the redneck and his buddies only hours earlier. With good reason this "good" Samaritan initially doesn't want to help his assailant. He'd prefer to leave him by the wayside.

But he helps him in spite of his feelings. The only delight he takes is bundling up Clem in a Gay Pride blanket and bringing him back to the gay bar to rest for the night.

What is instructive is that good feelings toward the people we help is not a prerequisite for being a good Samaritan. It is challenging to help people in need, especially if it means endangering our own lives. But Christ challenges us to help our enemies. Liking those we help has nothing to do with it. This is worth bearing in mind when we are asked to help the Iraqis, or North Koreans, or Serbs, or whoever happens to be our newest enemy.

5. Mental Baggage

> After this the Lord appointed seventy others and sent
> them on ahead of him in pairs to every town and place
> where he himself intended to go. ... Carry no purse,
> no bag, no sandals; and greet no one on the road.
> (Luke 10:1,4)

The priest had arrived from the Midwest to assist the
pastor of a parish in midtown Manhattan. He had never
been to New York City and was looking forward to spending
the summer in a church located in the theater district. He
suspected his stay would be very different from teaching in a
seminary. But he wasn't naive. After fifteen years as a priest,
he knew the importance of gathering as much information as
possible to minister to the locals: the prostitutes, street
people, con artists, addicts, and the poor. However, the
church's location in the theater district also meant that people
from all over the country attended liturgies before or after
they had gone to a play.

Since he wanted to be thoroughly prepared, he asked the
pastor for some words of advice. Little did he know how much
advice he'd get. He listened carefully as the pastor warned
him about the con artists visiting the rectory and telling sad
stories which they hoped would convince some unsuspecting
visiting priest that they needed financial help.

5. Mental Baggage

"If they ask you for a subway token to return to New Jersey, that's a sure sign they're conning you," the pastor warned.

"Why New Jersey?" the priest inquired.

Throwing his hands in the air, the pastor sighed, "I don't know! It's always New Jersey! The point is the money you give them they'll use for booze. Remember what I'm telling you! If someone tells you he's from out of town, has lost his wallet, and needs cash to get home, he's fooling you! No money, understand?" The priest nodded. The pastor added a footnote. "By the way, this kind of a con artist is smooth because he'll ask for a specific amount, say, $25.63, because the request sounds so much more authentic than $20.00 would. But don't be taken in! No siree! Don't be taken in!"

"No, no, I'll be careful," the priest promised. He took out a little notebook and wrote all of it down for future reference.

The pastor wasn't finished. "And be careful when you answer the door. You never know if you're dealing with a drug addict or someone who's a little short of a full deck."

The priest didn't need the last piece of advice. He'd already discovered that there were some very strange people in the city. Earlier that morning a young man had knocked at the rectory door. No sooner had the priest opened the door than the man proudly announced, "I am the Messiah and I've just married Barbra Streisand. We're going to be crowned king and queen of the universe by the pope. Then we'll rule from Jerusalem!"

The priest hardly knew how to respond. It would be too harsh to say "That's ridiculous!" and too nosy to ask how much Barbra knew of the situation or what the pope thought.

So he settled for, "How ecumenical!" And he added, "Why don't you take the day off and go the beach?" In hindsight he didn't think his advice made much sense, but the man seemed pleased and waved good-bye. The priest knew he'd have to be much better prepared for the next one.

At their next meeting he told the pastor, who shook a finger and said, "These people can be very dangerous. It's best not to let them into the rectory."

The priest decided that it would be best not to tell him about the other visitor. Another man had knocked at the door and asked if he could speak privately about a spiritual concern. The priest invited him into the sitting room and asked how he could be of help.

"Do you have visions of Mary?" the man asked.

"No, not that I can recall," the priest answered. "Do you?" He knew he shouldn't have asked that question because the man began talking about visions that would have put Joan of Arc to shame. Then he suddenly turned the conversation to something that deeply troubled him. He told the priest he was upset because every time he entered a church he was asked to leave. The priest was afraid to ask why, but he did.

"I suppose it's because I carry a sword into every church I attend," he said calmly.

"Oh," the priest said, trying to reflect the mood of the moment.

I don't understand why people would be upset about something like that, do you?" the man continued, as if wielding a sword in church were an ordinary occurrence.

39

Searching for words of wisdom, the priest finally said, "Well, look at it this way. If you go into church carrying a sword, you are likely to upset people. But if you join an organization like the Knights of Columbus, it's perfectly acceptable. You'll be invited to enter as many churches as you'd like!" Not wanting to neglect the man's question about visions, the priest added, "As for your visions, you may want to follow a saint who has visions rather than have your own. Otherwise people will think you're crazy." This wasn't exactly the wisdom he had hoped to impart, but he hoped it would help. "Does this make sense?"

"It makes perfect sense. I wonder why I hadn't thought of that!" And without a word more he got up, thanked the priest, walked to the door and let himself out.

Although the priest kept this story to himself, the pastor had more warnings. "From now on when someone knocks at the door, open the small grille and observe who's standing there. If you think the person looks suspicious, dangerous, eccentric, or even too normal, close the grille and don't open the door!"

The priest wasn't amused when the pastor told him that the confessionals in the church had escape doors, just in case. But he continued to write all of this advice in his notebook.

Next, the pastor told him to keep an eye on anyone who stood too close to the poor boxes. "You never know who's going to break into them. I've heard of men dressed as nuns jimmying the locks and running off with hundred of pennies from heaven!" He stopped for a second and continued. "As for the carpet at the main altar, roll it up after you've finished celebrating Mass, and when you're ready to celebrate, unroll it, and return it. We've already had a couple of our Oriental rugs stolen. And then they try to sell them back at a reduced price!"

Finally the pastor left to attend a parish meeting. The poor priest had more mental baggage than he could handle. He didn't know how he'd minister effectively to the people who came to worship at the small church.

Two days later, after presiding at an early morning liturgy, he was removing the chalice from the altar to lock it in the safe. Out of the corner of his eye he noticed a man dressed in a T-shirt, baggy pants, a rope belt, threadbare trousers and shoes but no socks. The man was waiting in the back of the church. Aware that the man's eyes were fixed on him, the priest didn't need to guess what the man wanted. Suddenly all the words of advice he had received from the pastor flooded into his mind. He hadn't even been approached by this man and he was already weighing the merits of his response. "No, we don't have any money to give," or "Yes we do but this isn't the time or place," or "We're definitely not giving any subway tokens to New Jersey," or "So you want to talk to me about God but that's not what's really on your mind!" As he tried to determine which answer would be most effective, the man approached him.

"Brother," the man began, "I need some money to tide me over."

No sooner had the words slipped from his lips than the priest selected an answer from his repertoire, "I don't have any. You'll have to knock at the rectory door for whatever you want." The priest was readying himself with another answer, when the man smiled and said, "The Lord be with you, brother."

Preoccupied, the priest muttered, "And also with you."

To which the man added, "And St. Mary and St. Joseph be with you."

Surprised at the man's answer, he was even more surprised as the man gently placed his hands on the priest's hips, planted a kiss on the priest's bald head, and laughed. At that moment the priest forgot the lines he needed to fit the occasion, laughed, and embraced the man. Then the man turned and left the church.

Within minutes the man returned, upset that there had been no answer at the rectory door. Once more he said, "I need some money to tide me over." And once more the priest struggled to recall what to say. He became defensive. Only this time he was so worked up, he swung his hands and arms as if he were preaching to a large congregation.

The man was amused as he stood watching the priest perform. Then he smiled broadly and said, "Brother, you get so dramatic!" He laughed, gave the priest a blessing, and merrily walked out of the church.

The priest was speechless. Slumping into one of the pews he thought about what had just happened. He recalled the passage from the Gospel in which Jesus told his disciples not to take any luggage with them as they went out to exorcize, heal, and bless the people they met on the way. He scratched his head. Who was carrying the luggage in what had just happened? Who had initiated the blessings? Who was doing the healing? Was it the priest with all his pastoral training and a mind filled with advice? In the end it was the homeless man who ministered to the priest. As he sat there thinking, the priest began to laugh. The laughter soon subsided as he sadly realized how long it had taken him to understand the heart of ministry.

Reflection

Jesus commissioned his disciples to exorcize demons and heal the sick. But he told them not to take any luggage with them. They were not to rely on self-help books, credentials, pills, notes, or designer clothes to carry out their mission. They were to heal others by being themselves, using their gifts, not using a bag of tricks.

The priest in this story is well intentioned, but he is gathering so much information to pack in his mental suitcase that he is unable to be fully present to the homeless man. He clings as much to his instructions as he would to any luggage. It is only when he forgets what he "needs" to remember that he feels free to laugh with his visitor.

When do formalities, traditions, and customs intrude in our relations with others by weighing us down with minutiae?

6. Upright or Uptight

Now he was teaching in one of the synagogues on the sabbath. And just then there appeared a woman with a spirit that had crippled her for eighteen years. She was bent over and was quite unable to stand up straight. When Jesus saw her, he called her over and said, "Woman, you are set free from your ailment."
(Luke 13:10–13)

It was the Sabbath. The elder at the podium waxed eloquently to his assembled brethren. "A clean, upright citizen! That's what we admire, that's what we desire, that's what we require. Anything less is downright unacceptable!"

"Clean 'n upright! Clean 'n upright! Clean 'n upright!" chanted the brethren enthusiastically.

"I shudder and tremble at the very thought of downright unclean folks contaminating our community," the elder continued. "A downright unclean citizen would wreak havoc. And what an offense to the upright, clean Holy One," he moaned as he beat his breast. "Consider the effect on our community if we were dirtied by unclean people," he warned. "Their very touch could be disastrous! Decent, clean, upright citizens marrying downright unclean foreigners would mean, would mean the end of discrimination as we know it!"

6. Upright or Uptight

"No, no, no," the brethren shouted as they pounded their foreheads with clenched fists. "We won't have it!"

On a roll the elder continued, "Or think what would happen if unclean, bleary-eyed beggars, bums, and blotchy-skinned lepers cast their shadows on us!"

"No, no, no!" the brethren cried again. But this time they were much more in sync as they pounded clenched fists on their foreheads while weaving backward and forward, signaling their horror over the elder's predictions.

"So my friends, I—" The elder stopped, caught off guard as he was ready to conclude his sermon. Peering over the heads of the brethren, he spied one falling asleep. "Straighten up, straighten up, I say," the elder bellowed to the wayward brother.

The person next to him jabbed him in the ribs and whispered, "Wake up! Wake up!"

Startled, the brother jumped to attention. Frightened because he had jeopardized a nearly perfect career of standing upright by regressing to a position that was a tad slanted, he begged forgiveness. "Oh, oh, oh! I'm so sorry. I've tried—I really have—to be upright, decent, clean. How can I make amends?"

"Yeah! Yeah! We get the point," the elder waved a hand. "Just don't let it happen again! Stand straight, shoulders back, chest out, tummy in, chin up!" Immediately the brother followed the elder's instructions. "Good! Good!" the elder nodded his approval.

Not deterred by the interruption he continued, "As I was saying, my friends, keep your eyes open. Remember it's our business to be upright and clean. We owe it to our families, to one another, and most of all to the one who has called us to be decent, clean, upright people. Of course I am referring to the Holy One, the Upright One, the Clean One whom we all adore! I thank you for your attention."

"Amen! Amen! Amen! Clean'n upright! Clean'n upright! Clean'n upright," the brethren chanted as they took their seats in the hall. They needed a few minutes of silence to savor the words of the sermon. His words encouraged and strengthened them to remain the clean, upright citizens they knew they were.

Once the service was over, others in the assembly were encouraged to speak about the Scriptures. No one noticed a young man step forward to the podium. But as soon as he began to speak, they leaned forward, cupped their hands to their ears, and strained to see who it was. "Oh no," they groaned, "not Jesus!"

Jesus began, "What does it mean to be upright? Certainly not uptight, my friends. Certainly not a fanatic about being clean, if by being clean we label others as unclean, unwashed, and unacceptable in our sight. No, this isn't what it means to be upright. I—" Jesus stopped as he noticed a figure huddled at the back of the hall. He waited a few seconds, then stretched out both hands, and invited the person to come forward. The person didn't move. Jesus waited a few more seconds. Once more he extended his hands, smiled, and gently called the person forward.

Slowly the person rose and began shuffling down the aisle. The brethren turned around. "Ohhh!" they gasped as they glimpsed who was coming down the aisle. As the person passed, those closest to the aisle hissed, "Keep your distance! Keep your distance!" They were shocked as an elderly lady, badly stooped and barely able to see where she was going, continued shuffling until she reached Jesus' side. She wore a tattered sweater over an old house dress. How she managed to dress and undress herself was anybody's guess.

Jesus took her hands. "My friend, how long has it been since you've been able to stand upright?"

"Eighteen years, sir."

"What's gotten you through the day all these years?

"Well, I just try to be honest. That's been a help." Pausing, she thought for a moment, chuckled, and added, "Oh yeah! I try to avoid that fella and his friends I just heard. Clean, upright citizens, you know! They can be pretty mean."

Jesus laughed. "Yes, they can be." The brethren in the front row grew restless and began grumbling. They were close enough to hear the conversation between Jesus and the unclean woman. Placing his arm around her, Jesus said, "You know, it's people like you who are genuinely upright." Then he addressed the brethren. "Yes, all of us can learn from this woman. To be upright is to be truthful. Can you be truthful?" he challenged them.

What no one noticed as he spoke was that ever so slowly the woman began to stand upright. "See, my friends! She is now upright in body as she has always been in her heart!" The woman smiled broadly and thanked Jesus over and over. He gave her a big hug as she stood tall and marched back to her place. But as she did, the brethren hissed as she passed them.

The chief elder shouted angrily, "You can't cure on the Sabbath. Cure on any other day, but not on the Sabbath!" What he really objected to was that Jesus had declared her upright on his own terms. This was bound to confuse the brethren and many other clean, upright citizens. They might also be confused about what the Holy One, the Upright One, desired.

"Sabbath or no Sabbath," Jesus answered. "She's a daughter of Abraham, and that means she's our sister. Don't you think eighteen years is long enough to be away from us?" The brethren didn't know how to respond. They were confused and upset by his words about what it meant to be upright.

But those members of the assembly who were not allied with the brethren and who had remained silent throughout the service clapped and shouted, "Right on, Jesus! Right on! You're downright upright about what's upright!"

Indeed! The Holy One must surely have breathed a sigh of relief that Jesus had finally set straight what it meant to be a clean, upright person.

Reflection

Upright is another word for *righteous,* but we rarely use the word *righteous* when we speak of someone being upright. The word *righteous* often suggests *self-righteous.* But in this story the upright person praised by the elder is really a self-righteous person. Of course the reason we've chosen to have the elder speak about upright, decent citizens is to contrast it with the woman who is stooped or bent over and therefore unclean. She lacks physical integrity and is described as being possessed by an evil spirit. She can't stand upright. However, Jesus points out that because she speaks from the heart, she is morally upright. On the other hand, the upright elder and the brethren are physically upright but morally bent because of their self-righteous attitude.

6. Upright or Uptight

Many people in Jesus' day associated a lack of physical integrity with sin. Recall the disciples questioning Jesus about the man born blind in John 9:1. "Rabbi, who sinned, this man or his parents, that he was born blind?"

We may think that we no longer associate a person's illness with a sin the person has committed. But we do. For example, if someone has contracted AIDS we may hear, "Well, he had it coming!" without even knowing the circumstances under which the person got the disease. Or if a person gets lung cancer, "Well, that person was a heavy smoker! He brought it on himself!" Or if a person has a heart attack and is overweight, we might hear, "She should have watched her diet!" We are not so crude as to speak of sin in these instances, but we may think the person "deserves" the illness as a punishment. If the person had led a clean life, he or she wouldn't be punished!

Jesus tries to set the elder and his brethren straight about what it really means to be upright. Are we able to look beyond the physical and mental ailments others have and see where genuine integrity resides—in their lives, not in the physical condition of their bodies?

7. Turning a Blind Eye

Then Jesus said to him, "What do you want me to do
for you?" The blind man said to him, "My teacher, let
me see again." Jesus said to him, "Go; your faith has
made you well." (Mark 10:51–52)

It didn't matter where they went. Myron panicked if he
thought Maude and his kids shouldn't see what was going
on around them. "Maude, look straight ahead! Kids, close
your eyes!" Then he'd whisper to Maude, "There's some
hookers on the corner. If the kids gawk at them, it'll be too
much for them. Who knows how they'd turn out?"

"Sure, sure," Maude and the kids dutifully answered.
However, as Maude looked straight ahead she raised her eyes
to the rear-view mirror to see what she was missing. As for
the kids, well, they cheated a little as they squinted to see
what was happening. "Big deal!" Junior muttered. The only
person who carried out the order perfectly was Myron. Hands
firmly planted on the steering wheel, he was determined to
focus on what was happening on the road, not on a shady
street corner.

Myron was on guard whether in the car or on foot. One day
while he and his family were walking down the street, his
eyes suddenly opened as wide as silver dollars. "Oh God!
Don't look now," he said. "Some guy's across the street

wearing a clunker of an earring, a ring in his nose the size of a horseshoe—and, and who knows what else he's got on his body! Well, I'll be. He's got something dangling from the back of his head."

"You mean a pony tail?" Maude asked.

"A pony tail?" Myron was astonished. He couldn't believe some guy would be perverted enough to wear some pony's tail. "Oh, what is this world coming to?" he moaned. He never bothered asking Maude how she knew the man was wearing a pony tail since she wasn't even looking at him. It didn't matter. What mattered is that he kept his family on the righteous path and look straight ahead. Had he been listening he would have heard "Big deal!" from one of the kids.

Repeatedly Myron fought to screen out whatever he considered unseemly for his wife and kids to notice. It could be teenagers with spiked orange hair and baggy pants. "Don't look! It might give the kids ideas!" Or, it could be a billboard ad from which men in underwear seductively stared down at Myron and his family. "Don't look up there! It might give us all ideas!" Or, it could be the homeless on skid row. "Don't look! You don't want to end up being a bum!"

Sometimes Myron unwittingly engaged in conversations with "those kinds" of people. One afternoon, he and his family stopped for ice cream at a family restaurant. A couple of beautifully dressed women were sitting in the booth directly across from them. They glanced admiringly at Myron and his family. Myron noticed them and managed a wink. When the women were ready to leave, they stood up. Myron was very impressed. "Boy, they're not only beauties, they're tall ones," he told Maude. "Looks like they could be Rockettes!"

7. Turning a Blind Eye

As he spoke one of the beauties walked over to his table and said in a deep bass voice, "You all look like such a nice family."

"You sure do," the other woman said in an equally deep voice.

"Well, thank—" Myron was going to say thank you but he had already put two and two together. "Exceptionally tall women with bass voices! Oh my God!" he thought. Turning quickly to his family he cried, "Maude, Sissy, Junior, Ralph! Get up! We're leaving *now!*" He threw some money on the table, jumped up, and herded his family out of the restaurant so fast that the beauties were left standing and staring.

"What's with him?" one of the ladies asked as she adjusted her well-coiffed wig.

"You got me!" the other answered, straightening her dress to ensure everything was packed in the right place.

"Those women aren't women—they're, they're men!" Myron whispered to Maude as he rushed his family away. "We can't let our kids see women who are men. They'll be confused about who's who!"

Maude closed her eyes. "Yeah! I'm sure this would really throw the kids into a panic."

And from the back of the car a low rumble, "Big deal!"

"What you don't see can't hurt you!" was Myron's motto. No wonder he had the statue of the three monkeys in his living room. One of the monkeys had his hands covering his ears, the second one's hands covered his eyes, and the third one's hands covered his mouth. "Hear no evil, see no evil, speak no evil!" Very nice words. But there was a problem. Myron had spent so much time screening out what was happening around his family that he ignored what was going on within his family.

Finally, Maude had enough. "Junior's been smoking pot!" she said.

"You gotta be kidding!" Myron answered.

"You're too busy looking the other way. You don't want anyone of us to see anything and you've turned a blind eye to your family," Maude told him. "Oh," she added, "I found a load of porno magazines stacked under a blanket in Ralph's closet. Just something else you haven't noticed by telling all of us to look the other way. I think you need to get some help."

"Porno! Pot smoking! What's going on? And what do you mean I need help?" a rattled Myron demanded.

"I mean go and see someone who can help you see what you've refused to see. Go and see Jesus Martinez. He's a social worker. He has an eye for what's happening around here."

Myron said nothing. He was shocked by his kids' behavior. He'd tried to be protective, but it seemed to have backfired. Maybe he did need help. So he made an appointment to see Jesus Martinez.

When he met Jesus Martinez, Myron was surprised. Jesus had only one eye. Jesus noticed Myron studying his face. "Yes, I have only one eye but I see more with this one than most do with two eyes. So let's drive around and see what you've been missing."

7. Turning a Blind Eye

First Jesus pointed out the kids strung out on drugs in a seedy neighborhood. He told Myron how many of them ended up on the streets because their folks never paid much attention to them or their problems while the kids were at home. "They just ignored them and left them on their own," he said. "So now they're here and they might die here."

Then he drove Myron to skid row and explained that many of these men had been highly paid professionals or happily married men. Then their companies downsized, and they couldn't find work. Their depression often led to alcohol, and just as often their marriages fell apart. Some of the homeless had been institutionalized for psychological problems and then released to take care of themselves.

"Take care of themselves! That's a laugh!" Jesus said. "How are they supposed to do that?" He looked at Myron. "Are these the 'bums' you didn't want your family to see?"

Myron didn't answer.

Later Jesus drove through a section of town where some of the "beauties" hung out. The looked like the women Myron had met at the restaurant. "As kids they were knocked around. 'Fairies,' their classmates called them. 'Fairies,' their dads called them as they threw them out of their homes. 'Fairies,' these kids thought when they had nowhere to go. 'Why not be a queen fairy and make some money?' they thought. You didn't think about that when you dragged your kids out of the restaurant as fast as you could, did you?" Jesus asked pointedly.

"No," Myron answered weakly.

"Nor did you see the male hustlers working the streets because they too were called queers, fags, and fairies. Because they were harassed, even by religious leaders who should have known better. They were treated as if they were a piece of meat. So they thought, 'Well, if I'm no better than a piece of meat, I oughtta try and make a buck selling myself as a piece of meat." Jesus paused as he thought about what he had said. He continued, "And that's all that most decent people see. Right?"

By this time Myron's eyes were wet. He didn't speak. But he had seen what he hadn't wanted his family to see.

"So as I said, Myron," Jesus continued as he drove him back to the center, "I see more with one eye than most do with two."

"Yeah! I guess you do," Myron nodded. When Myron got out of the car, he thanked Jesus for helping him to see. "Jesus, I think I'll go home now. I think I'd like to see what my kids are up to. I don't want to turn a blind eye again. I think we'll go for a ride. I want to see whatever there is to see. You've helped me. But I may be back. I need you, Jesus!"

"Sure thing! Anytime, Myron, anytime!"

Reflection

"Turning a blind eye" means we don't want to see what there is to be seen. Of course we must have some idea of what it is we're ignoring; otherwise, why would we turn away? We've read about the Serbs in Kosovo who, just as the Germans during World War II, turned a blind eye to the atrocities being committed all around them. Ignorance enables us to plead innocence and so excuse ourselves from responsibility for what is happening. Turning a blind eye to these situations also allows us to live with ourselves because we don't see the tragedy unfolding. For example, if we clearly saw the pain in the face of a loved one who was suffering because of something we were becoming (e.g., an alcoholic), then we might be unable to live with ourselves unless we changed.

In this story Myron thinks that, by ignoring those things that might adversely influence his family, he can protect them. But since his refusal to see and acknowledge the problems around him diminishes his vision, he doesn't see what is happening in his own family.

If we make a practice of ignoring whatever inconveniences or causes us pain, what we see in the world around us will continue to diminish. The consequences of turning a blind eye is that we isolate ourselves within our own world, systematically excluding what is "unclean" or "impure" from our lives. We are no different from the purists in Jesus' day. And like those purists we fail to exercise the virtue that will help us see again. That virtue is compassion.

8. Irene

From there he set out and went away to the region of
Tyre. He entered a house and did not want anyone to
know he was there. Yet he could not escape notice,
but a woman whose little daughter had an unclean
spirit immediately heard about him, and she came
and bowed down at his feet. Now the woman was a
Gentile, of Syrophoenician origin. She begged him to
cast the demon out of her daughter. (Mark 7:24–26)

Irene was desperate. Her daughter had been acting
strange for weeks. She'd sit in her room without saying a
word all day long. Staring into space, she seemed to be in
another world. She wouldn't answer any questions and she
barely touched her food.

"Paula, Paula, you've got to go outside and get some fresh
air," Irene urged her daily. But Paula wouldn't budge.
Perhaps she was possessed by a demon. Irene was not the
kind of woman who'd sit back, wring her hands, and do
nothing. A spunky, strong willed Greek woman, she had
overcome previous adversities when her husband died after a
long illness. He seemed to suffer from the same demon that
possessed her daughter. Irene never gave up hope as she'd
sing his favorite songs to him and dance around his bed
seductively in a gown she'd worn at their wedding fifteen
years earlier when she was twenty pounds lighter. But to no

avail. When he died, she vowed she'd get back at the demon if it ever entered her life again. And it did.

Irene decided that if her daughter wouldn't go outside and get fresh air, Irene would carry her outside. Since Paula was only twelve, Irene was able to carry her outside and place her in a wagon she had a neighbor build for Paula. She propped her up with pillows and began pulling the wagon through the busy streets of the village every day. Irene did everything she could to arouse her daughter's interest on these daily trips. She'd make funny faces to get her to laugh, or do a waltz step for a couple of minutes in the village square, or sing a favorite song. The villagers were amused by Irene's efforts, but Paula didn't react to anything Irene said or did.

"Girl, I don't know what I've got to do to get you going. But I haven't given up and I won't. Maybe a doctor can help." Irene didn't have too much confidence in doctors. They hadn't been able to help her husband and they cost more than she could afford. "I'll worry about money later," she thought. So she brought Paula in her wagon to a doctor. The doctor examined Paula and concluded that Irene ought to put her away with girls who had similar problems. "Maybe she'll feel at home with them," he told her.

"At home? Are you crazy? How would you like to be locked up?" she said as she grabbed the handle of Paula's wagon and marched out of his office.

When she visited another doctor he suggested that Irene shake her violently an hour each day. "Why?" an astonished Irene asked him.

He told her it was his professional opinion that whatever was ailing her would get dizzy and leave her daughter as a result of this treatment. An indignant Irene answered, "Shake her up? I'll shake you up. Then let's see if what's ailing you gets dizzy and leaves. If it does, then I might try the treatment on Paula. Shake her up! Indeed!" Once more Irene grabbed the handle of Paula's wagon and marched out of the office.

A third time she went to a doctor. And his proposal? "Submerge her up to her neck in ice water for an hour twice a day. It's shock therapy. The ice water will shock whatever is bothering her and it will leave."

Irene couldn't believe what he was proposing. "Submerge her up to her neck in ice water? Do you think I want a popsicle for a daughter?" she asked.

"Just a suggestion," he muttered as he saw the wild look in Irene's eyes.

"Yeah! Well, you might consider dunking your head in ice water and see what happens," she said tartly as she hauled the wagon out of his office and slammed the door behind her.

Irene had hoped that visits from friends and relatives might help Paula. When Paula was well they used to come over and play with her. But now?

"I've got arthritis in my feet. I can hardly walk. Sorry, I can't come," Irene's sister said.

"Yeah! Yeah!" Irene thought. "She's got arthritis in her head too!"

"Sorry I can't get over to see Paula," Irene's brother said. I've got arthritis in my back."

8. Irene

"Is this arthritis some kind of epidemic or what?" Irene wondered.

She got the same excuse from her twin cousins. "We're so sorry but we've both got arthritis in our knees. We couldn't possibly come."

Irene wasn't buying these excuses. "Arthritis in their knees! How convenient! Arthritis in all four knees? Between the two of them there must be only one brain. They ought to be able to think up their own excuses." She sighed. No help from the relatives. Where could she turn? Who could help Paula get well?

Soon she would find out. One day she decided to take a stroll by herself. Given Paula's condition Irene didn't fear her daughter would jump up and leave the house while Irene took her walk. So she walked and walked and walked until she was on the outskirts of the village. Normally there would have been a few persons traveling by foot on the edges of the village. But surprisingly a small crowd had gathered in front of a small house about a hundred feet off the road. Curious, Irene walked over to the house and asked one of the persons in the back of the crowd, "What's going on?"

"Oh, that Jew we've heard so much about is staying in this house. He's the fella who's supposed to have healed his kind on the other side of the border. We don't think he'll do anything for us—we're not his kind of people. But we'd like to see what he looks like. However, he doesn't answer the door when we knock."

Irene rolled up her sleeves, elbowed her way through the crowd, and started banging on the door with both fists. Without waiting for an answer, she opened the door and stood facing a startled Jesus. He had been trying to find some peace for a couple of days. He had told his friends, "I really need to get away. I've been very busy and I need some peace and quiet." Now he was facing what appeared to be a very strong-willed lady. "Hmmm! I wonder if all these people are like her."

Now that Irene had made her grand entrance, she was speechless. She hadn't anticipated facing a foreigner that afternoon. Nor did she think she'd ever barrel her way through a crowd and force her way into a house as she had. But if he was a healer and could do something for her daughter, then what she had done might be worth it. No longer speechless she took a step forward and fell on her knees. Before Jesus had a chance to say anything, she pleaded, "Sir, my daughter's got a devil of a problem. And I don't know what to do about it. From what I've heard, you've got the power to do something about it! So I'm begging you—do something about my daughter. I've tried everything and nothing works."

Jesus was speechless for a moment. This woman wasn't wasting any time making her point and asking for help. But he had decided early on in his career that he wanted to help his own people. He didn't want to be bothered with foreigners' problems. He wondered how he could get his point across. Seeing how determined she was, he knew he'd have to be pretty blunt. "I'm gonna be honest with you," he began. "What comfort I have to give, well, I've pretty much decided to give to my own people."

Irene looked up at him. "C'mon now! You can do better than that! Excuses! Excuses! I've heard too many of them."

"Boy, this is a tough one," Jesus thought. "Well, let's put it this way. You don't take food that's meant for children and give it to the dogs." He knew this was strong language, comparing the Jews with these foreigners, but ....

"Not bad! Not bad, sir. But you can do better than that. After all, even the dogs get the leftovers!"

Jesus was caught off guard once more but this time he was delighted. "Great comeback!" he cried. She wouldn't let go! She was spunky and she really believed in him. "OK! OK! You win! When you go home your daughter is going to be waltzing around the house!"

"Oh! Thank you! Thank you!" Irene was smiling through her tears.

"By the way, what is your name?" Jesus asked.

"Irene!" she answered.

"Irene! Wow! Really? If I understand my Greek, "Irene" means "peace." Am I right?"

"Yes, it does," she answered.

Jesus lifted Irene to her feet and embraced her. "I came to find peace and peace came to me, but not as I expected it," he said. "And I've learned something else today. I've got to reach out to a lot more folks besides my own people. Thanks Irene and peace be with you!"

Irene was ecstatic as she waved good-bye. She galloped all the way home. When she opened the door, she burst into tears of joy as she saw her daughter waltzing and laughing in the living room. Finally her daughter was healed.

As for Jesus, he had found peace in a most unusual way.

Reflection

Irene is a foreigner and her daughter is possessed by a
demon. So, according to the purity laws, Irene has two strikes
against her: She's unclean because she's a foreigner and her
daughter is unclean because she is a foreigner and possessed.
But Irene is a persistent woman who doesn't take no for an
answer. In this remarkable scriptural passage from Mark, we
get a glimpse of a very human Jesus who shows signs of
prejudice in his remarks to a Gentile woman. Nowhere else do
we have a picture of Jesus showing prejudice yet breaking
through his bias by granting the woman's request to cure her
daughter. In the story, as in the scriptural passage, Irene is
determined to have the day. And she does.

The scriptural passage illustrates in a marvelous way that
Jesus' growth in wisdom (Luke 2:52) did not stop when he
reached adulthood but continued in his adult life. This story
also ought to be an example for us that the Jesus we confess
as Lord has gone before us stumbling along the way and
learning through his stumbling the meaning of being human.
In his encounter with this feisty Greek woman, he learned
with a touch of grace what it meant to be everything to
everyone.

9. Absurd*

They brought to him a deaf man who had an impediment in his speech; and they begged him to lay his hand on him. He took him aside in private, away from the crowd, and put his fingers into his ears, and he spat and touched his tongue. Then looking up to heaven, he sighed and said to him, "Ephphatha," that is, "Be opened." And immediately his ears were opened, his tongue was released, and he spoke plainly. (Mark 7:32–35)

"Yeah! Yeah!" These words and a few grunts were about the only response Moshe ever gave to anyone. "Can you lend me your ear for a moment?" his wife would ask. "Our son is having a difficult time in school."

"Yeah! Yeah!" Moshe waved a hand as he sat cutting his nails or working on a puzzle. Then his wife would pour her heart out about their son's problem. As she spoke, Moshe's only reaction was "Yeah! Yeah!" Every now and then he'd look up from his puzzle or doodling, act as if he were listening, and throw a few more grunts her way. But his wife knew she should never have asked him to lend an ear because now as so many other times he gave her a deaf ear. "Yeah! Yeah!" she'd mutter under her breath and leave the room.

---

* From the Latin root *surdus,* meaning "dull, deaf, insensitive."

9. Absurd

It didn't matter who visited Moshe or what they asked him. His response was always the same. Over the years he had developed a pattern of not listening, and it didn't change—except his responses were becoming absurd. For example, when a friend visited to tell him that her mother had died, Moshe's answer was, "Fine, I'll make a note to call your mother tomorrow."

"But she's dead!" the friend said.

"Well, then I'll send her a note the day after tomorrow."

"How absurd!" his distraught friend thought as she left Moshe.

His wife was deeply hurt when she told him she didn't feel well and he answered, "Yeah! Yeah! That's great news. It ought to happen more often. Why don't you work on it?"

"What do you mean? Are you crazy?" she asked.

"Huh? Oh I mean I think the trip will do you good. Yeah! Yeah!"

"Moshe, you're absurd!"

"Yeah! Yeah!"

He was becoming absurd at work too! "Moshe, we've been given the day off tomorrow. It's a lovely day to go to the beach. Isn't that great?" one of the workers told him.

"A day off! You mean it's winter already?"

"Winter? Moshe, it's the middle of the summer!" The worker scratched his head and walked away wondering if Moshe were

9. Absurd

going crazy. "How absurd!" he thought. "Does Moshe have a hearing problem?" he asked another worker. Others were asking the same question. "Can Moshe hear? He isn't making any sense." Of course, he had never listened to their concerns, no matter how serious they were. Moshe would utter, "Yeah! Yeah!" and if he were really up to it, "Oh! Is that so?" But they never came away feeling he had heard them.

At home, at work, everywhere people who knew Moshe were more and more alarmed at his inane responses. They described Moshe's answers as absurd, simply absurd. Finally his co-workers had had enough. They went to their manager and complained, "He's given a deaf ear to everything we say. His answers make no sense!"

"Send him to me!" the manager ordered. "I'll talk to him."

"Moshe, the boss wants to see you. Now!" Moshe didn't answer. "I said the boss wants to see you right now."

"I can't hear you," Moshe said as he cupped a hand to his ear.

This time the worker shouted, "THE BOSS WANTS TO SEE YOU NOW!"

Moshe shrugged his shoulders, "I still can't hear you!"

Shocked, the worker marched into the manager's office and told him that Moshe was deaf, stone deaf. Immediately the manager rose from his chair and went to see for himself. "Moshe, can you hear me?" Seeing that Moshe couldn't hear, the manager cried, "CAN YOU HEAR ME?" Now Moshe was alarmed. He could see the manager's lips moving but he heard nothing, absolutely nothing.

9. Absurd

"We can't keep him here if he's deaf. What are we going to do with someone who's deaf?" the manager said matter-of-factly. Turning to one of the workers, he asked her to write a note to Moshe telling him that he could no longer work at the plant. That the manager could make this decision with such indifference was partly due to Moshe's own chronic indifference toward everyone he worked with. His insensitivity had not endeared him to his fellow workers when they needed an understanding ear. But the manager's easy dismissal of Moshe was also due to the fact that Moshe was now dispensable. After all, he wasn't a whole man anymore, just a deaf person. So Moshe returned home.

His wife and kids didn't know how to help him. Since he had so often given them a deaf ear when they needed him, they didn't feel Moshe's condition was any different than it had been. Actually they felt relieved because they didn't have to listen to his absurd responses to their questions.

But in the weeks that followed, they felt obligated to bring him to whatever doctor might be able to help him. The doctors' diagnoses were varied. "Too much wax in the ear," one doctor concluded. But after the doctor removed the wax, Moshe was still deaf.

"He just has a bad head cold. That's all! His ears are plugged up." But Moshe didn't have a cold at all.

"Too much water in the ear from swimming!" another doctor concluded. But Moshe had never gone swimming in his life. "Maybe he submerges himself in his bathtub," the doctor suggested. Now who was absurd? Moshe was obviously discouraged as he trekked from doctor to doctor. He was also more and more frustrated. He couldn't even hear himself mutter. Deprived of hearing, all he could do was observe others closely as they spoke. This was all new to him since he had never bothered paying any attention to the people around him when he could hear.

In the weeks and months that followed, Moshe began to read their lips and their body language. It was as if a whole new world was opening up to him. He noticed his children laughing or crying. And he paid careful attention to his wife's activities throughout the day. When he took a stroll outside he marveled at young lovers holding hands and embracing one another, children skipping down the street, trees swaying in the wind, birds flying gracefully in the blue sky. His reaction to what he was seeing was childlike wonder. His response to the world around him brought joy to family and friends who hadn't gotten any response when Moshe could hear.

One day a stranger visited Moshe. He had heard about Moshe and was interested in helping him. Known throughout the countryside as a healer, by everyone except Moshe, the stranger's name was Jesus. "Another one of those doctors!" Moshe sighed. But Jesus did not signal to Moshe that he had any intention of following in the footsteps of the doctors who preceded him. He simply observed the way in which Moshe paid attention to him. He seemed to be more interested in Moshe's sensitivity to what was happening around him than in healing his hearing problem. But then looking directly into Moshe's eyes, Jesus said, "Moshe, I can help you hear again, but I cannot promise you will continue to notice others as you do now. What I can promise is that if you listen with your heart and eyes as you are doing with me, you will never turn a deaf ear to others again. Clearly you have learned something you could only have achieved through becoming deaf. Whatever you decide is up to you."

Everyone in the room was startled by Jesus' comments. They wondered why they had asked him to visit Moshe if not to heal him of his deafness. Moshe knew the consequences of not being able to hear again, but he also knew that he had learned to listen to others as he had never listened before. As the days passed he had become more and more sensitized to the world around him. If his life had been reduced to absurdity when he could hear and now was filled with meaning because he listened in a new way, would being physically healed add any more meaning than he now enjoyed? He thought for a minute or two and then looked at Jesus. "I know what I must do, Jesus. I thank you for your words. I know the path I must take." Jesus smiled at him, blessed him, and left the room.

Though deaf, Moshe never turned a deaf ear to anyone again. He lived his life lending an ear to anyone in need.

Reflection

"I read you" is an expression we use when we tell someone we understand what he or she is saying. It's an interesting expression because "reading" means more than hearing. It also involves "seeing." To read someone is to pick up visual as well as audial cues from the person. We notice facial and bodily movements, which help us listen to the person. We can gather whether the person is tense or at ease. We can realize what we can't on a telephone, that is, if the person is giving us his or her full attention. When we hear a person talking to us, we get much more information when the person is physically present.

Try talking to someone who's watching television or working a crossword puzzle. Notice how his or her attention is divided between you and the activity. If the person doesn't give you his or her full attention, you may feel as if he or she isn't really listening to you. If this goes on day after day between persons, the chances are they are becoming deaf to each other's concerns.

Saying persons have become deaf to one another's concerns isn't meant to demean the hearing impaired. As our story develops, Moshe learns to listen to others even though he cannot hear them. Being absurd is the result of not listening. We've all had moments when we've given stupid responses to others because we haven't really listened to them even though we've heard their words.

In Jesus' day a deaf person was considered unclean and an outsider. Jesus' healing activity consisted in healing the person's illness, which medical anthropologists (Crossan 81) distinguish from curing a disease. Healing an illness is a psychosocial phenomenon in which the alienated person feels as if he or she now belongs to the community. Curing a disease is medically treating the disease. This distinction is easily understandable if we think of persons who have AIDS. They might receive good medical treatment but not be welcomed by parents or relatives. Integration into family life would mean they were being healed of an illness, even if they still had the disease. Some scholars doubt that Jesus cured diseases, but they don't doubt that he healed illnesses. This debate is not our concern. The point is, healing is more important because we all need to know that others care about us. And this doesn't necessarily happen if we've been cured of a disease.

In this story Moshe decides that he doesn't need to have his disease cured because his illness has been healed. Jesus tells Moshe he can cure the disease, but Moshe might revert back to his old ways of turning a deaf ear.

We should ask ourselves: Are we so preoccupied with our concerns that we refuse to listen to others? The first step in

9. Absurd

discerning whether we are becoming absurd is to listen to ourselves listening to others.

10. Unbelievable

He came to his hometown people and began to teach
the people in their synagogue, so that they were as-
tounded and said, "Where did this man get this wisdom and these deeds of power? Is not this the
carpenter's son? Is not his mother called Mary? And
are not his brothers James and Joseph and Simon
and Judas? And are not all his sisters with us? Where
then did this man get all this?" And they took offense
at him. But Jesus said to them, "Prophets are not
without honor except in their own country and in
their own house." And he did not do many deeds of
power there, because of their unbelief. (Matthew
13:54–58)

Ike and Jake, elders of their assembly in Nazareth, had
preached eloquently for years from the podium in their
assembly hall. Everybody in the town had spoken highly of
them. All one needed to do was walk down any street and
hear comments about them like, "Wise! Witty! Inspiring!
Mesmerizing!" Of course Ike and Jake basked in the
compliments they received daily as they strutted down the
streets of their town.

Whenever they preached from the podium, each pretended
not to notice the members of the assembly commenting
approvingly on his homily. But Ike and Jake lived for these
compliments.

And of course their families benefited as well. "My, but it's such a privilege to be admired as Jake's wife," Miriam proudly told Ike's wife, Sarah.

"And I will tell you, Miriam, I feel like the Queen of Sheba herself being Ike's wife," Sarah sniffed. "I have much to be thankful for."

"Me too!" Miriam quickly added.

And they did. Neighbors often brought them freshly baked foods as a sign of respect and gratitude for the positions they held as wives of these two prominent elders.

Always the neighbors would say to one wife and then the other, "Your husband is unbelievable! So gifted! So ... so, I'm speechless!"

Then one day Jake and Ike got word that Jesus was coming to town. They had heard it was Jesus' hometown, but they simply couldn't recall having heard of him. All they knew was his reputation as a healer and a remarkable preacher. They looked forward to his visit to the assembly hall.

"Unbelievable!" Jake whispered to Ike as they listened to Jesus preach from the same podium they had preached so often. "I could listen to him all day."

"Yes, unbelievable!" Ike echoed Jake. "I'm glad he's come home to visit us." As they looked around the assembly hall they noticed that there was a capacity crowd who had gathered to hear Jesus that evening. What was equally obvious was how enraptured the crowd was as they listened to Jesus' words.

10. Unbelievable

Over and over Jake heard people whispering. "Can you make out what they're whispering?" Jake asked Ike.

Ike listened intently for a minute. "'Unbelievable' is what I'm hearing," Ike reported.

Now Jake strained to hear what people were whispering. His face darkened as he looked at Ike, "Yeah! That's the word they're using—unbelievable. But I'm hearing more than that. I'm hearing, 'Jesus is the best we've ever heard in this assembly hall!'"

"Nooo," Ike said. He found it unbelievable that the folks would say that this Jesus was the best they had ever heard in their hall. "Maybe we haven't heard right. Is it possible that they like him better than, than—"

"Us!" Jake added ominously. No sooner had he said "us" than they heard a loud round of applause for Jesus. And it was noticeably louder and more sustained than either had ever heard for themselves. There were even shouts of "This man is something else! Where did he get all the smarts he has? He's too good to be true!"

Ike and Jake looked at each other. "Do you know what this means for us? If he decides to stay here permanently?" Jake asked Ike.

"Do I know? I can guess and what I'm guessing isn't good," he answered.

"We'll be second bananas!" Jake said.

"Who will look up to us?" Ike panicked.

"Or bring our wives fresh bagels?" Jake wondered.

"Or treat them like queens?" Ike worried.

"Queens?" Jake couldn't think straight.

"Our wives! Our wives!" Ike reminded him.

"Oh yeah! But what are we gonna do?" Jake asked.

As they sat there, they heard a man in back of them whispering to his friend, "To think that his dad is one of those simple-minded carpenters and his mom takes in washing to make ends meet. Why, the whole family lives in that dumpy neighborhood just east of here. It's unbelievable that they have a kid like Jesus, isn't it?"

"Hear that?" Jake whispered excitedly.

"Yeah!" Ike whispered back. The idea was already being hatched. "Jesus comes from poor trash. I know what those folks are like. They're out of work half the time."

"Well, well, well, so what we're seeing in front of us is a fake!" Jake relaxed now that he had something on Jesus. "I'm betting he's memorized someone else's material."

"Right! And knows how to put on a good act!" Ike was putting two and two together. "I'll hand that much to him."

"I will, too," Jake conceded. "But he can't get away with it. We won't become second bananas to a con artist! No sireee!"

Jake and Ike became more and more agitated as Jesus spoke. And when the crowd gave another round of applause for Jesus, Jake and Ike opened fire. Jake cupped his hands to his mouth like a megaphone and shouted, "Who's your mom?

10. Unbelievable

Isn't she the one who takes in the dirty laundry? And your dad? He's out of work half the time, isn't he?"

Then Ike joined in. "So how is it possible that you're Mr. Smarts doing such great things for us? I'd say you're a con artist!"

At first the crowd was stunned by what they heard, and they were silent for a moment. But when they realized it was their respected elders who had spoken, elders whom they had trusted, then they too began to raise questions. "Yeah, come to think about it—you're too smooth," someone yelled.

"Pulling the wool over our eyes!" another chimed in.

"A charlatan!" still another shouted. Right and left people began to cry, "Unbelievable!"

Jesus shook his head sadly as he looked at the crowd. Speaking as loudly as he could above the insults coming from them, he said, "Why is it that others can accept me for who I am and what I do but you can't. So my mom takes in the wash and my dad hasn't got the best job in town. What difference does it make if they live where they live? If this means you can't accept me, then there isn't anything I can do for you." Then he left the podium and walked out of the assembly hall as the crowd continued their attack.

Jake and Ike breathed a sigh of relief. They didn't need to worry about Jesus anymore. As they got up to leave, a number of people thanked Jake for exposing Jesus as a charlatan. They added that they thought Jake was the most respected and best loved elder they had in the assembly. Ike was visibly upset as he stood there while Jake received the compliments. Jake was ecstatic, until a number of persons approached Ike and told him how much they appreciated his saving them from being taken in by a con artist. And they added that as far as they were concerned no one came close to being as eloquent and charismatic in the assembly as he was. Ike was overjoyed but now Jake was visibly upset.

When all the people had left the assembly the two men were standing alone, facing each other. Jake glared at Ike. "I suppose you think you're the cat's meow— charismatic, eloquent, the best, huh? Well, we'll see!"

Then Ike shot back. "And I suppose you think you're top dog because you've been called the best loved, most respected elder, huh? Well, we'll see!"

And without a word more, each left the assembly hall through different exits.

Unbelievable, huh?

Reflection

Ike and Jake's desire to torpedo Jesus' success at preaching to their congregation ultimately works against them as they end up fearing each other's being the most liked preacher in the congregation. Each man has lived for his own honor and gloried in the adulation of the villagers. But self-promotion can breed unhealthy competition, and this competition means someone is going to end up being a nobody. No genuine community can exist where self-interest is the main concern.

In this story the whole community loses because two men decided that Jesus had to be the nobody. But when people are intent on their own aggrandizement at the expense of others, the community is in danger of collapsing into a gathering of isolated individuals fearful of becoming nobodies themselves.

10. Unbelievable

Jesus cannot help people if they insist on depriving others of the right to be somebody in order to achieve success. This is not the kind of community Jesus intended when he preached about the reign of God. What would he say to us today about some of our own attempts to exalt ourselves at others' expense? What would he say about careerism within the ordained ministry where cardinals, or bishops, or priests try to achieve positions of power within the church?

11. The Crackpot

Then some people came, bringing to him a paralyzed man, carried by four of them. And when they could not bring him to Jesus because of the crowd, they removed the roof above him, and after having dug through it, they let down the mat on which the paralytic lay. (Mark 2:3–4)

You're a crackpot," his wife bellowed, "a real crackpot!" This wasn't the first time Minnie had gotten so worked up. She had been married to Morris for fifteen years and each year they were married she had become increasingly frustrated with his crazy schemes to make money. "You tell me you don't want to earn a living like everybody else. You want to be different. Well, you're different all right, but your crackpot ideas have gotten us nowhere, nowhere," she sobbed. What had gotten her so upset?

This time it was more than his plan to mass-produce specially designed earmuffs for men who were tired of listening to their wives' harangues. A year earlier he had invested a considerable sum of money in the project, but only a few courageous or foolhardy husbands bought the earmuffs. He thought he'd try again but this time he'd add a bonus and hopefully get rid of a couple hundred earmuffs gathering dust under their bed. And the bonus? Lip clips for the wives!

11. The Crackpot

Minnie wanted to clip Morris' lip with an upper right to the jaw!

Morris never thought of himself as a crackpot. "I'm an entrepreneur," he'd tell prospective financiers. Years earlier he had convinced the owner of the local winery to buy waterproof booties for his employees who crushed grapes with their bare feet in the huge vats. Unfortunately, after a couple of days' sloshing around in the booties, the employees rebelled. They loved the feel of the grapes on their bare feet, and they resented wearing booties. Besides they leaked anyway.

Morris wasn't deterred by this minor setback. He forged ahead and capitalized on the growing number of muggings and robberies occurring in the wilderness outside of the village. He succeeded in interesting a friend in financing the production of a line of cheap traveling tunics that would be sprayed by pet skunks. The idea was that potential robbers would keep a respectful distance from the travelers as they got a whiff of their eau de cologne. However the pet skunks resented being ordered to spray on demand, and they turned on Morris's defenseless employees. Before the mutiny, the few tunics they had sprayed not only kept the robbers at bay but also caused the travelers to faint in the noonday heat. Needless to say Morris's friend never spoke to him again.

But Morris was not one to give up. These and other failures seemed to feed his appetite to earn a pile of money with his crackpot ideas. More and more of the villagers began referring to him as the village crackpot, out for a fast buck. But there were enough slow-witted persons around who seemed ready to buy anything from anybody, including Morris. For example, why would anyone want to consume more than two Ex-Lax tablets at a time? Since Morris had added the taste and color of jelly beans to the tablets, he advertised that customers would want to consume them by the handful. The foolhardy rushed to buy the tablets and they ended up doing a lot more rushing after they gobbled up their handful. No wonder Minnie was beside herself.

"All right! All Right! I'm sorry, Minnie. I'm sorry! No more earmuffs, no more lip clips!" But Morris was already secretly planning his next project, which he was convinced would give him the respectable name recognition which he needed. He was going to produce gloves—not pairs of gloves. The selling point: "Say you lose a glove. Since it didn't match the other, there'd be no reason to throw away the one that's left. You just go and buy another one that doesn't match. See! No need to buy matching gloves at all!" He'd be rolling in the money if he could get this project financed. He didn't want to tell his wife about his new idea since she wasn't presently disposed to accept any of his ideas.

He knew he had to act quickly before she got wind of what he was doing. Once he had begun the project, she could hardly step in and stop him. She'd get angry, slam the pots and pans around the kitchen, but she knew from past experience she couldn't stop him.

As he hurried down the street to his office, he didn't notice the villagers arching their eyebrows and shaking their heads as they muttered, "What a crackpot!" Then an irate villager caught sight of him, ran up, and intercepted him. "You're a crackpot!" he cried. "Jelly bean–flavored tablets, indeed! I couldn't leave my house for ten days because of you and your crackpot ideas. Now I'm out of work because I couldn't explain to my boss what happened. And even if I could have explained I would have been too embarrassed." Then unexpectedly he shoved Morris so hard that Morris fell to the ground. Angrily the man stormed down the street without bothering to look back. When Morris tried to get up he couldn't. He appeared to

11. The Crackpot

be paralyzed. Fortunately a few villagers saw what had happened, and managed to carry Morris back home.

Although Minnie was distraught when Morris told her what had happened as he lay on his mat, she was surprised that something like this hadn't happened years ago. She held her tongue though, because he was already in enough pain.

In the following days Morris's condition didn't improve. Minnie called in the doctors but they didn't know what to do for him. One of the doctors who had fallen for one of Morris' crackpot projects coldly suggested that Morris would come up with some crazy idea to help himself. But Morris didn't have any ideas. Not this time. If he needed to think of some new idea to make an extra buck, he'd always come through. But this was a different situation.

About two weeks later, a couple of friends visited him and they had a suggestion. There was a well-known healer in town by the name of Jesus. He was staying with friends not too far from Morris's house. "Suppose we bring you to him. Maybe he can help. What d'ya say, Morris?"

Morris had heard of Jesus. He knew Jesus had his own ideas on life—some of which sounded like crazy ideas to the religious authorities in the village. He smiled. Well, if Jesus had been accused of crackpot ideas, that alone endeared him to Morris. "Sure fellas, why not?

So his friends gently lifted him on his mat and carried him to the home where Jesus was staying. There were so many villagers gathered outside the house that it was impossible to enter through the door. Now what were they to do? Although Morris's body was paralyzed, his mind was still very active. "Fellas, we've got to get me up to the roof. Then we can

remove some of the tiles and lower me down through the
opening."

One of his friends muttered, "Here we go again." But any
idea was better than none. "So how do we get up to the roof?"
he asked.

"Hmmm," Morris thought for a minute. "Go next door and
ask if we can borrow a ladder. Tell the person we'll give him a
free pass to my Dates 'n' Nuts Oasis for Weary Travelers. Just
don't tell him it's in the middle of the desert!"

His friends shrugged their shoulders. "Might as well try,"
one of them said. "We've nothing to lose."

Ten minutes later two of his friends returned with the
ladder. "It worked! It worked!" they said. One of the friends
laughed as he said, "That guy was excited about the prospect
of going to a Dates 'n' Nuts oasis. He didn't even ask where it
was."

Immediately his friends set the ladder against the house
and carefully managed to lift Morris and his mat up the
ladder to the rooftop. Once on the roof, they carefully removed
five or six tiles from the center. As they peered inside the
room directly beneath them, they spotted Jesus through the
shower of dust. Surprised at what was happening above him,
Jesus looked up as a shaft of light illumined the room. Not
waiting for an invitation, Morris's friends dropped the ladder
slowly into the room. Then they managed to lower Morris and
his mat down to the ground.

Jesus' eyes twinkled as he looked at Morris lying on his
mat. Glancing upward at the opening in the roof and the
crazy way Morris had gotten into the room, Jesus laughed
heartily. He asked, "What's your name?"

11. The Crackpot

"Morris Muskovitz."

"Ah! I've heard about you, Morris. Are you the one they call a crackpot?"

"Yeah! Yeah!" Morris sighed. "I'm the one."

"So you're out to make a fast buck, huh?"

"Well, something like that," Morris conceded. He thought Jesus was being blunt, but he couldn't deny that this was what he had been about most of his life—even if he hadn't been very successful.

"Do you think you can start putting some of your ideas to work for folks who've got it pretty bad in this village?"

"Well, I, I," Morris looked directly into Jesus' eyes. He had heard that Jesus was accused of being a crackpot by his enemies for helping folks who were in bad shape. Maybe he could give it a try too. "I guess I could."

"Good!" Jesus answered. Then placing his hands on Morris' head he gently said, "Your sins are forgiven you!"

Some of the people in the room grumbled. They complained that Jesus didn't have the right to do what he was doing.

Jesus looked sharply at them, "Oh yeah? Well, just so you know I do." He turned to Morris and said, "Morris, stand up, pick up your mat, and go home." Morris froze. "C'mon Morris. You can do it!"

Morris felt a tingling sensation in his back. Slowly he lifted himself to a sitting position and then rose to his feet. He

11. The Crackpot

couldn't believe what was happening to him. "Thank you, thank you, Jesus," he muttered.

Jesus looked at him and said, "Remember! The next crackpot ideas you get—they're to help others. OK?"

"Sure thing!" Morris answered.

"Good-bye then!" Jesus turned to help others who had come to be healed. Morris and his friends walked out of the house. His friends could tell that Morris was up to something. But what? In the following weeks they'd find out.

Morris was thinking of designing a beauty parlor for poor widows to attract potential husbands.

He wanted to create resorts specially designed for the blind so they could listen to heavenly music.

He also wanted to create resorts specially designed for the deaf so they could feast their eyes on heavenly sights.

He thought of creating safe havens for prostitutes to protect them from abusive patrons. He thought he'd also like to help them use their makeup skills in the cosmetic business.

But what he wanted to do most of all was design tablecloths embroidered with expressions like, "No one's a stranger at this table. Everybody's welcome!" because he knew that Jesus wanted everybody around the table whoever they were.

Minnie thought that was the biggest crackpot idea of all. But Morris wouldn't back down on that one. He knew if it was crazy, he was in the same camp as Jesus and that was OK with him.

89

Reflection

We don't know if Jesus was ever called a crackpot or its equivalent by his contemporaries. However we do know he was accused of being a drunkard and a glutton and of being possessed by Beelzebub. At one point in his career, his own family wanted to restrain him because people were saying he was going crazy (Mk 3:21). Obviously the religious elite considered him a dangerous crackpot; otherwise he wouldn't have been crucified.

If we didn't know who had given us the Beatitudes, we might have concluded it was a person who was out of touch with reality. Even knowing it is Jesus, we might wonder if what he describes as fortunate or worth celebrating (e.g., being persecuted) sounds more like advice coming from a crackpot rather than a sage.

Religious, scientific, and artistic geniuses are often thought to be crackpots by their contemporaries and only later are recognized as geniuses. What is normative behavior for the members of any society is often the yardstick used to determine who is well adjusted and who is crazy.

Morris is a crackpot whose ideas are considered crazy. But his genius for coming up with strange ideas serves him well once he meets and is healed by Jesus. He undergoes a conversion. His ideas might still seem like those of a crackpot, especially to his wife, but now they are more in line with Jesus' crazy ideas about what God's reign would look like if more people like Morris joined Jesus in helping the nobodies become somebodies.

12. Family Values

Soon afterwards he went on through cities and villages, proclaiming and bringing the good news of the kingdom of God. The twelve were with him, as well as some women who had been cured of evil spirits and infirmities: Mary, called Magdalene, from whom seven demons had gone out, and Joanna, the wife of Herod's steward Chuza, and Susanna, and many others, who provided them out of their resources. (Luke 8:1–3)

"Do not think that I have come to bring peace to the earth; I have not come to bring peace, but a sword.
    For I have come to set a man against his father,
    and a daughter against her mother,
    and a daughter-in-law against her mother-in-law;
    and one's foes will be members of one's own household. (Matthew 10:34–36)

He had just finished preaching and was speaking to a few people who had stayed behind when he saw a woman standing a short distance away. He guessed she might want to speak to him. After he had clarified a point about honoring one's parents, the others left, and he beckoned the woman to come forward. She hesitated.

"Woman," he called. "Did you want to talk to me?" She remained silent.

Finally, she said, "Yes Rabbi, I would like a word with you."
But she didn't move. It seemed as if she couldn't quite decide
whether she really wanted to speak to him.

Jesus waited patiently. "Come," he said. "You can talk
freely!" He wondered if she were afraid of saying what was on
her mind. Since she was wearing her chador, or veil, he could
not see her face. Slowly, however, she limped forward, and
when she was within a couple feet of Jesus she removed her
chador.

Jesus moaned. Her eyelids were partially closed and her
face was badly bruised. The chador served to protect her from
the eyes of those around her, but she wanted Jesus to see her
without the covering. Now Jesus was silent. For a moment he
could say nothing. When he had regained his composure, he
asked, "Woman, what is your name?"

"Susanna, but please don't tell anyone we've spoken," she
pleaded. She was nervous and frightened as she quickly
looked over her shoulder to see if anyone had followed her.

"No, I promise I'll say nothing," Jesus said.

"Thank you, Rabbi," she said. "I listened to your sermon on
the commandments. But I have a problem with them."

"You're not alone," he said. "Most people do." He sensed
that there was a connection between her problem and the
bruises that disfigured her face.

Her voice trembling, Susanna forced her words, "How can
one be obedient to one's father when that father abuses his
daughter?"

"You mean when the father punishes his daughter by beating her?" he asked.

"Yes, yes," she said, and then almost imperceptibly, "and more than beating her."

This wasn't the first time Jesus had had a painful conversation of this kind with a woman. When he heard the words, "and more than beating," he knew how difficult it must be for her to describe what she meant. So he helped her. "By 'and more' do you mean that your father violated you?" Aware of how sensitive this matter was, he added, "You needn't say anything. Simply nod if what I say is true. Otherwise do nothing."

Another stretch of silence. Finally tears forming in her eyes, she nodded. Jesus sighed. Again it had taken place within a family. Families were tightly knit. Belonging to a family gave its members an identity and status. Ostracized from the family, the members became loners, anonymous unless they became attached to a group that could serve as a family. It was no wonder that those living within the family clung to it even if it meant abuse. And since family life was dominated by the powerful father, this kind of abuse was an ever-present possibility.

Head lowered, the woman standing before Jesus had been violated and deeply shamed by her father. Jesus was surprised Susanna had come to him and told him as much as she had. By coming forward, she was exposing both herself and her father. She was shamed and he had dishonored himself. Although she had done nothing to provoke her father's assault, she still suffered deep shame for what he had done to her.

"Susanna," Jesus asked. "Does this happen often?"

12. Family Values

"Yes, Rabbi."

"How do you manage to survive these assaults?"

"I try to think of something else when he has his way with me. I tell myself I am somewhere else and that this is happening to someone else's body. At other times I do whatever I can to avoid him. But you can see on my face what happens when I resist. What you don't see are the bruises on my body."

"No, I don't," he said. But he guessed she limped because of her father's harsh treatment. What she described he had heard from women with similar stories. Often their stories came to light after he had performed an exorcism. Then he discovered that sexual abuse had given rise to the woman's possession. The chilling voices of the demons were the abusers' voices continuing to haunt these women.

Fear in her eyes, Susanna cried, "What should I do? What can I do?"

"What would you like to do?" Jesus asked.

"Leave my father's house. His word is law. No one there dares to defy his authority. My mother remains silent and the others wouldn't think of crossing him."

"But if you leave where will you go?"

"I don't know, I don't know," she whispered. "I have nowhere to go. No one will accept me. I'll be nobody once I leave the house."

Jesus felt both anger and compassion. He was angry because he didn't think God intended the stronger members

94

of a family to dominate the weaker and destroy them in the process. He felt compassion because God was a Father who embraced the weak and the strong as being one family, only if they respected and looked after one another. Kinship based on blood ties often proven inadequate to ensure what this Father desired of his children. Only those who chose to do his Father's will by treating one another with dignity could avoid a family life that could be so destructive.

Jesus asked Susanna where she intended to go if she left her family. Now he would make an offer. "Join us! Other women, Magdalene and Joanna, are with us. If you join us, however, it means committing yourself to helping others like yourself who have been abused. If you decide to be a member of our family only one will matters and that is God's."

Susanna's tears flowed freely. She knew how angry her family would be, but she could risk it if it meant she no longer had to endure the abuses she had suffered in the past. What appealed to her was Jesus' challenge to help others suffering from similar abuses. "Yes, I want to join you, Rabbi!" she said enthusiastically.

"Good! My friends are now your brothers and sisters. They'll support you in every way possible."

While he was talking, another small crowd was gathering around him. He hadn't intended to preach anymore that day, but his conversation with Susanna energized him to speak. He looked out at the crowd. Did they expect comforting words? If so, they'd be disappointed. This time his words wouldn't be comforting. "Do not think that I've come here today to speak about bringing peace to this earth. I have not come to bring peace but the sword. For I have come to set a man against his father, and a daughter against her mother, and daughter-in-law against her mother-in-law, and one's foes will be members of one's household. Whoever loves—" He hadn't gotten far into his sermon when someone interrupted him.

"Your family is way in the back and your mother wants to talk to you."

Jesus' family had already heard villagers gossiping that he had been savaging family values a couple of days earlier when he preached. They were concerned that he was angering too many important people by attacking traditional family values. But they also knew their own reputation was on the line since whatever he said reflected on them. They decided they had to restrain him from further attacks because the word was spreading that Jesus might be losing his mind. This news propelled them to high-tail it to the outskirts of the village where he was preaching.

Jesus thanked the person for the message from his family. But he wasn't about to talk to them now. What inspired him to add a few more words to what he had already said was their claim on him based on blood ties as well as Susanna's story. Turning once more to the crowd he said, "Who are my mother and my brothers?" And looking at those around him, he said, "Here are my brother and sister and mother. Whoever does the will of God is my brother and sister and mother."

Briefly he looked toward the back of the crowd to see if what he said had any effect on his family. They were wildly flinging their hands in the air. They weren't pleased. He made a mental note to invite them to a special party where they could meet more brothers and sisters than they knew they had. All his brothers and sisters, including Susanna, might convince them that having more siblings wasn't such a bad idea. He ended his short sermon by reassuring the crowd that he hadn't come to destroy families.

Honoring father and mother was still a priority, but God's will of who belonged to God's family was the message Jesus continued to preach passionately. He would preach it to his dying day. Little did he know that indiscriminately bringing together men and women from every strata to break bread at the same table inevitably would lead to his death—all because he gave new meaning to family values.

Reflection

In discussions on family values we hear little about Jesus' observations on family life in his own day. Dominic Crossan (58–59) has pointed out that there were many abuses in family life in Jesus' day. The families were patriarchal and the father governed with absolute authority. The weaker members of the family could be abused within a system in which the father wielded the authority. And biblical scholar Steven Davies (86–89) makes a strong case that many exorcisms Jesus performed were on persons whom we now refer to as having Multiple Personality Disorders. Based on his transcultural study of this phenomenon, he concludes that these disorders are and were the result of sexual abuses within the family.

Jesus savaged the family structure that made these abuses possible. As in this story, such abuses reduced the abused to a nobody who was powerless to do anything to avoid abuse. Jesus preached that the healthy family was made up of persons (related or not related by blood) who did the will of his Father.

Today men, women and children within families still suffer from emotional and sexual abuse that is dehumanizing and causes untold suffering. Any member who is abused becomes a nobody in his or her own eyes.

Does Jesus challenge us to be more aware of these problems within families and call us to do whatever we can to be supportive of agencies that provide services for the abused so they can regain their dignity as somebodies?

13. Peter's Dilemma: How Many Times?

Then Peter came and said to him, "Lord, if another member of the church sins against me, how often should I forgive? As many as seven times?" Jesus said to him, "Not seven times, but, I tell you, seventy-seven times." (Matthew 18:21–22)

Peter's mother-in-law, Momma, was steaming. "Peter, what do you think I'm running? A food pantry? Sure! Jesus heals me as I lay sick with a fever. So it makes me happy that I can cook a delicious meal for such a nice boy. Fine! This I can do. But no sooner am I on my feet than you've got me sloshing around the kitchen, cooking food to feed half the town! I'm delighted that so many should want to see Jesus, but a food pantry I'm not running. Did you have to tell everybody in the town he was here? A big mouth you have. That I cannot say for your brain."

Peter was hurt by his mother-in-law's outburst, especially in the presence of his father, who was visiting them, and his other family and friends. It was humiliating to endure her scathing comments. For several days he wrestled with whether he ought to let it go or attack her as she had him. Revenge would be nice, but he knew it would be better to forgive her. Maybe she just wasn't thinking when she berated him in public. He decided that even if he had a big mouth, he had a bigger heart. "Momma, let's be friends again. No more name calling. I'll forget how you treated me. Shall we shake on it?"

"OK! OK!" Momma muttered. She stiffly thrust out a hand to Peter and then hobbled off to help her daughter with the housework.

No sooner had Peter made peace with her than Momma was at it again. "A big mouth you have. That I cannot say for your brain. So what do I say when your Poppa pops in here on his way home from fishing. Wheww! A three-day beached whale he smelled like. What do I say? 'My, such a lady's man you are! That eau de cologne you're wearing—such a catch you'll get!'"

Peter was furious. She had sprayed a deodorizer in the room, not once or twice but three times during his father's visit. Adding insult to injury, she did it while wearing a clothespin on her nose. Even though Poppa pretended not to notice, Peter knew Poppa must have realized he wasn't welcome because he left the house ten minutes after he arrived. How could he have missed the point as Momma circled him three times like a shark waiting for the kill?

"Momma, that's my Poppa you humiliated. You spray him and it's the same as spraying me!"

That seemed to be the cue Momma needed as she grabbed her assault weapon, and cried, "Oh yeah! So you're reminding me I didn't finish the job?"

"Now Momma," Peter covered his face. "Calm down, calm down." His mind racing, Peter tried to figure out how he could calm the troubled waters. Maybe he had been too harsh on her. Perhaps the room did smell like a fish market. Inhaling deeply, he decided it did. Maybe Poppa needed to be told that whenever he left the fish the fish didn't leave him. "You have a point, Momma. It's OK! You can put down the canister. I'll see to it that Poppa cleans up before he visits us again. Shall we shake on it?"

"Hmmm," Momma stood there wondering if she should put down the canister or bop Peter on the head with it. But since her son-in-law didn't want to hold a grudge, she slowly lowered the canister onto the table and stiffly extended a hand to Peter. After they quietly shook hands, Momma silently left the room as if nothing had happened—or so it seemed.

"Wow! Wow! My mouth is hot as an oven! What did you put on that fish?" Peter cried as he downed several glasses of water to put out the fire. His wife and kids couldn't figure out what Peter's problem was as they sat around the table. Their fish was mildly spiced and tasted delicious. Since Momma had prepared the meal she was the only one who could explain what happened.

"Well, you asked me to put cayenne pepper on your fish!"

"What? I didn't say cayenne. I said can yeh pepper my fish?"

"Oh!" Momma paused to think about that. "Well, my hearing's been getting worse lately. I though you said cayenne. So what's the harm? It'll clear your sinuses."

"I don't have a sinus problem."

"Who knows? You could one day. Nothing like a trial run with the cayenne!"

"Oy vey!" Peter wanted to help Momma to a dose of cayenne pepper. "No, no, no," he muttered. "Mustn't get nasty. Got to forgive her. We need peace in this house. Peace! Peace! Peace!" His face still flushed from the cayenne, Peter decided to go along with Momma's weak explanation for slipping the cayenne on his fish. "OK! OK! Momma, I forgive you. But please get your hearing checked at the doctor's. Maybe you've got too much wax in your ears." Or, he thought maybe there was nothing between her ears. But he suppressed the thought—it wasn't very forgiving!

Momma smiled sweetly. "I think a little rest is all I need. But thank you for your concern. It isn't like you. You're improving. Now let me get you a little more fish."

Peter quickly covered his mouth with a napkin. "No, no, Momma!"

She laughed. "Do you think I'd use more cayenne pepper? What do you think I am? A sadist?"

A good question. For in the days that followed Momma continued to intentionally or unintentionally create havoc in Peter's life. On one occasion she took all his tunics to wash at the local stream. But this time she beat his tunics with a large stone for so long (mercilessly, one might say) that the tunics were nearly in shreds. "It's my eyes," she explained when Peter confronted her. "I'm never sure when I've got the dirt out. And as you know, I don't care to leave any spot unstoned. So, I overdo it!"

"Yeah! Yeah!" Peter grumbled as he sported cleanly shredded tunics. "So I might be setting a trend. Who knows?

Nothing like air-conditioned tunics on hot days." He tried to put the best spin on what had happened. And once more he looked for reasons to forgive what she had done. "Maybe her eyes aren't all that good! How should I know?" And he forgave her.

But no sooner had he forgiven her for beating the tunic out of his tunic than she had pulled up all the flowers he had planted around their little house. "Sorry," she apologized, "they looked like weeds. Better you should get flowers that look like flowers."

Next she tossed a large bag of bread crumbs on their front lawn, and hundreds of pigeons flew in and feasted on the crumbs. "Sorry," she apologized, "who knew there could be so many pigeons in Palestine?"

Then she smeared a sticky molasses-like substance on the soles of Peter's sandals. "Sorry," she apologized, "just thought it would prevent you from stumbling—a safety feature you might say."

And Peter's reaction to all this? He fumed, gritted his teeth, moaned, paced the floor but bravely, courageously, managed an "I forgive" each time his mother-in-law turned his world upside-down. Is it any wonder that when he had the opportunity he went to Jesus as fast as his sticky sandals would permit? Bypassing the customary greeting, he blurted, "Lord, when my brother (but he really meant mother-in-law and didn't want to smear her good name), when my brother wrongs me, how often must I forgive him? Seven times?" Peter was convinced he had gone the limit, done the heroic. He was proud of himself. He had managed to do what most folks he knew would never have done—forgiven his mother-in-law not one, not two, not three, not four, not five, not six, but seven times. He had pulled it off! He was sure Jesus would give him a pat on the back, maybe even a medal.

Jesus smiled. "Ah," Peter thought, "it's coming, it's coming!"

"Seven times, Peter? No, not seven times. I say seventy times seven times."

"What?" Peter's mouth dropped open. "But that's impossible, Jesus. I've done a yeoman's job. I've been a success in forgiving seven times. And I'm washed out!"

Jesus laughed. "Maybe you're trying too hard. Maybe you think it's all up to you. Like this is some kind of game where you win or lose points. You forgive—then you're a winner and you feel great about yourself. You can't forgive—then you're a loser and you feel guilty about yourself. It's as if forgiving were all up to you. No room for God, is there?" Jesus paused. Then quietly, "Why don't you stop trying so hard? Seventy times seven. That's four hundred and ninety times. Of course, it's impossible for you, little you. But there's someone bigger than little you in this. Think about it!"

Peter searched Jesus' face for something more definite. "Give it a rest, Peter. You're thinking too hard. It'll come to you. Now what do you say we take a walk? By the way, is there something wrong with your sandals? Looks like you got something sticky on them." Peter didn't know what to say. All he knew was that he didn't have to be in a rush to forgive anybody—and he didn't have to feel guilty about it.

Reflection

Although Jesus' healing touch was the way he welcomed the alienated back into the community, we read in Matthew that the followers of Jesus were asked to forgive those who had offended them. Reconciliation was to occur in this fashion. In the scriptural passage for this story, Peter asks Jesus how many times he is to forgive someone who has offended him. Is seven times enough? Jesus gives Peter an answer but the answer raises another question. How do we go about forgiving someone so many times?

We know from our own experience that forgiving someone who has deeply betrayed us only once seems like a Herculean task. It might even seem as though too much is being asked of us. Jesus' response to Peter is a "pastoral" response, which we might suggest to someone who finds the task of forgiveness overwhelming, especially when the task refers to forgiving someone within one's own family (e.g., a mother or father who has been physically abusive). Jesus' response in this story is based not on his words in the scriptural passage but on what he might say given his understanding of the circumstances in which people find themselves. This is a pastoral response.

Forgiving someone who has deeply offended us might seem overwhelming because we assume two things. One assumption is that if we manage to forgive, we will have succeeded. The other assumption is if we can't forgive, we will have failed. The emphasis on what we have to do places the burden of forgiveness squarely on our shoulders. Maybe we are expecting too much of ourselves and too little of God in assuming the heavy burden of forgiveness. Does the story suggest another gentler, less burdensome way of being a forgiving person?

14. Company Boys

John said to [Jesus], "Teacher, we saw someone casting out demons in your name, and we tried to stop
him, because he [is not of our company]." But Jesus
said, "Do not stop him; for no one who does a deed of
power in my name will be able soon afterward to
speak evil of me." (Mark 9:38–40)

"We're company boys, not anybody's boys, not anybody's
toys, we're company boys," John crooned as he, Jim,
and Peter strolled down a dusty road outside the village
where Jesus was staying.

"And mighty proud we're company boys," Jim added. "We
were nobodies until Jesus came along. Sure we hauled in tons
of fish while we worked for Poppa on the boat. But now we've
made it big!"

"Yep!" John agreed. "We're hot stuff now that we're hangin'
out with THE MAN."

"Hot stuff! Right on!" Jim shook a fist. "Can't you tell that's
what folks are thinking when they see us? They're so
impressed they're almost breathless when they greet us."

Peter jumped in. "That's what happens when you're a
company boy. People stand up and take note. They admire the

way our guys have bonded. 'A tight knit group,' you hear them saying. And we are. One for all and all for one! No one's out of step. Yep! We're company boys all right," Peter concluded.

"And no one's gonna break up that old gang of ours," Jim warned.

"Together forever, and ever, and ever," John promised.

Overjoyed, they belted out their theme song:

> We're company boys
> Not anybody's boys
> Not anybody's toys
> We're company boys.

But as they sang and rejoiced, they noticed a huge crowd had gathered about a hundred feet ahead of them off the side of the road. Jim smiled. "I bet the other fellas from our company are there wowing the crowd. Letting the folks witness for themselves what a great company we've got."

"You bet!" John said. "Seeing what a neat little club we've got going for us. In fact, I can hear one of our guys doing a healing act. Do you hear?"

The others listened intently as they heard the words, "In Jesus' name I say be healed!"

"Yeah! It's one of ours," Jim agreed. "Oh boy! Our outfits gonna be in neon lights before we know it. Can you see it? 'Make Way! Make Way! Jesus and Company Is Coming Today.' Let's join our buddies and show the folks what Jesus' full company's like!"

So Peter, Jim and John trotted over to the back of the crowd, and stretched to see which one of the brothers was performing. Peter whispered, "Is that Phil?"

Jim whispered back, "No, I think it's Matt."

But John whispered, "I'd say it's Bart." As they continued guessing which of the disciples might be doing the healing in Jesus' name, it slowly dawned on them that whoever was healing in Jesus' name wasn't a company boy.

"No! I don't believe it. It can't be," Jim gasped.

"I'm speechless," John gulped. "Really, really, really speechless!" Well, not quite speechless.

"I'm, I'm, I'm, I'm, I'm," Peter was speechless.

Finally Jim spoke the words none of them wanted to hear, "He's not a company boy!"

To which John groaned, "He's not even a he. He's a she!"

"He's a she?" Peter said weakly and fell to the ground. "He's a she. A she," he muttered as Jim and John helped him to his feet.

Jim wondered, "If he were a he who's not a company boy, that would be bad enough. But he's a she! Woe is me! What are we gonna do about it?" Obviously disturbed at what they had discovered, he took his hankie and patted at the beads of perspiration forming on his bald head.

John found his voice. "I know what we'll do. We'll march through this crowd and demand that she stop what she's doing. We'll tell her she's not a company boy—never was, never could be, and she doesn't have the right to do anything in Jesus' name. We're an all boys club. And that's that!" Such authority!

"Good idea," Peter blurted. "We've got to set her straight! Boys will be boys. It's our company."

"Agreed!" Jim said. It was unanimous.

The three barreled their way through the crowd until they were face to face with the woman who was healing an elderly man. "You can't continue doing good unless you're a company boy," Jim demanded.

Startled, the woman looked at Jim and asked, "What are you talking about? I can't heal unless I'm a 'company boy'? Are you crazy?"

"Am I crazy? Do I sound crazy? I'm simply telling you our company has the rights to healing in Jesus' name. Nobody's gonna do any good in his name except us. And why? Because we're COMPANY BOYS, THAT'S WHY!" And as if by reflex Peter, Jim, and John proudly, courageously belted out:

> We're company boys
> Not anybody's boys
> Not anybody's toys
> We're company boys.

By this time the crowd was getting angry. "Sounds like you're crazy to me!" someone shouted.

"Yeah! Off the wall!" another agreed.

"Tutti Frutti," someone else shouted.

"Go home!" everybody chimed in.

The three men began feeling that they had walked into a lion's den as the crowd grew more and more hostile.

"Calm down! Calm down!" the woman cried, waving both hands to the crowd. "Listen fellas! I think you better go before they carry you out. And one more thing. Tell Jesus what you've seen and heard here."

"Yeah!" an elderly gentleman added. It was the man whom the woman had healed. "Tell him he oughtta be happy he's getting some help. Maybe he can get a little R and R now."

"Oh!" Jim was beside himself. "C'mon fellas! Let's get out of here and tell the boss what's going on here." The three marched through the crowd but they let everyone know who really belonged to the company.

> We're the company boys
> We're not anybody's boys
> We're not anybody's toys
> We're the company boys.

When they returned to the little house in the village where Jesus was staying, they marched into a small room. Jesus was resting on a sofa. "Jesus! We've got bad news! Real bad news!" John thundered.

"Bad news? What bad news?" Jesus asked.

"We found someone who doesn't belong to our company who was healing someone in your name. We told her she didn't have the right to do this. She's not a company boy. She's not even a he. Just a she!"

"Wait! Wait!" Jesus interrupted. "You tried to stop someone from doing good because she's not with us, and especially because she's not a he?" He paused. He didn't know whether to laugh or cry. "What do you think I'm running, fellas? A mutual admiration society?"

"Well—" Peter began.

"Some kind of club for a privileged few?" Jesus was on a roll. "And those few being the 'boys'? C'mon! C'mon! That's the very thing we're against. Have you forgotten we're out to do away with No Admittance signs in this country? Anybody who wants to do good in my name—I'm for that person. Besides, I could use a little more help. I need some R and R from time to time."

When the three men heard Jesus mention R and R they looked at one another. At that moment something clicked. "Yeah!" they said. A little R and R would do Jesus a world of good. And the more they thought about it, the more they realized the world could do with good wherever it came from. Then and there they realized they needed time to think over how they had acted. And as the days passed they realized whoever did good could accompany them. No longer did they think of themselves as the company boys. And that was fine with Jesus.

Reflection

Cliques or in-groups have existed for centuries. As this story shows, there was even a tendency among Jesus' disciples to form a clique. If this could happen among Jesus' first followers, it can certainly happen in our churches. Parish councils and committees, priestly gatherings, pious organizations, liberals, and conservatives are all susceptible to becoming cliques.

Cliques exclude people regarded as undesirable because they don't think or act in the same way as the members of the clique. A tyranny of uniformity exists within cliques that makes them unhealthy. Some of the groups that might have formed cliques in Jesus' day were the Pharisees, Sadducees, scribes, and Herodians.

Since cliques don't welcome diversity, they are mutual admiration societies in which the members see themselves mirrored in one another and like what they see—themselves. Seeing themselves in one another confirms the individual's identity within the group. Take away that confirmation and the person is likely to be very insecure.

Jesus' mission was to invite people from all walks of life to open fellowship at the table. He sought to break down barriers, not create new ones. This was a tall order since people who form cliques want to keep the barriers in place.

The challenge for us is to follow Jesus in refusing to exclude others from enjoying full membership in Jesus' family, which includes all who do the will of his Father.

15. Going Fishing

When [Jesus] had finished speaking, he said to Simon, "Put out into the deep water and let down your nets for a catch." Simon answered, "Master, we have worked all night long but have caught nothing. Yet if you say so, I will let down the nets." When they had done this, they caught so many fish that their nets were beginning to break. (Luke 5:4–6)

Peter was on a fishing expedition. Of course, he wouldn't have called it that. To him this would have sounded too, well, fishy. But consider!

Peter was twenty-five, not bad looking but not a knockout either. Slightly shy but not inarticulate, he could hold his own in an intelligent conversation. Having recently graduated from college he taught math at the local high school. Peter had a few close friends with whom he partied, went to movies, and occasionally to a baseball game. He loved to read mystery novels as well as the classics and had read *Moby Dick* two or three times. As far as romantic interests? Well, he was looking but hadn't found anyone he was interested in. And since he was slightly shy, an aggressive approach to getting the right catch wasn't appealing. The bar scene turned him off, and the women he admired at school were already married. Shopping malls and food stores seemed inappropriate places to meet a potential mate. "I'd be hauled in as a stalker if I hung out at the malls," he laughed as he told a friend.

Then how was he to meet anyone with whom he could be romantically involved? This was on his mind one Sunday evening as he approached the church where he regularly attended evening services. Entering the church he slipped into a pew about ten rows from the back of the church. No sooner had he sat down than he happened to glance across the aisle. "Holy Mackerel," he gasped as he spotted a woman who was a real knockout. Then and there he fell for her hook, line, and sinker! "I've got to meet her. But how?" he wondered. Since he wasn't the kind of guy to cross the aisle and say, "Hi, my name is Peter. Shall we get together for a tete-a-tete after Mass?" he knew he had to use a different kind of bait. But what kind?

He decided that the following Sunday evening he'd show up an hour early at the front of the church, wait for his beloved to appear, "accidentally" bump into her, and voila! He'd then exude oodles of charm and apologize for being so clumsy. And to secure her interest he'd wear designer clothes, use some mint breath spray, rub Obsession on his cheeks, and Old Spice under you know where.

So the following Sunday he shows up an hour early at the front of the church, smelling like a rose garden. He waits and waits and waits for the gal of his dreams to appear so he can "accidentally" bump into her. As it happens he bumps into everybody but her. The church bells signal the service is about to begin and he's still standing outside, a lonely sentry, waiting for her to show. Dejected that she hasn't shown up he drags himself into the church. And guess what? There she is, ten pews from the back of the church. He scratches his head. Of course! "Damn," he mutters, then quickly neutralizes the "damn" with a sign of the cross. "She entered through the side

116

door." Unfortunately he hadn't thought about the side doors when he planned where he'd do his fishing.

Still he manages to maneuver himself into the same pew—with about four people in-between. Obviously she doesn't notice him. But everybody else does. "Phewww!" someone mutters. With all that Obsession, mint breath spray, and Old Spice, folks are bound to pick up the scent! Still the evening's not a waste. At the exchange of peace, he manages a stretch that torpedoes past four startled parishioners as he touches the fingers of the one he adores. No matter that she can't even see whose fingers are touching hers. Given the circumstances who could ask for anything more? He cast the line and got a nibble. That's something! But she hasn't taken the bait—not yet! Elated, he glides home and winks at himself in the bedroom mirror. The expedition is underway.

The following Sunday evening it's Obsession, breath spray, and Old Spice all over again! On his way to church he plots how he'll draw her attention. He's savvy enough to know that he's got to canvass front *and* side entrances as he waits for her at the church. He also realizes this will be a bit taxing as he moves quickly from entrance to entrance.

At the church he puts his plan into action. What he hadn't calculated was her ability to change her appearance so dramatically. Different hairdo! Different makeup! So when she arrives, she slips right past him.

Exhausted from running to and fro, he once more drags himself into church. Finally he spots her where she usually is—the tenth row from the back! "So, she's gotten away again," he moans. But this doesn't deter him. Immediately he spies an empty spot in the pew directly in front of her. All the while mumbling, "Scuse me! Scuse me! Scuse me!" he climbs over five parishioners to the place in front of her. And when it's the time to give a peace greeting, he turns to her, smiles broadly, shakes her hand, sighs, and shakes her hand again. Then he casually points to the lapel of his jacket where he has pinned a card with his name, address, and telephone number. She smiles, then turns to the folks in back of her to shake their hands. But Peter sighs, "Ah! That smile!" Another nibble! And that's it for this Sunday's liturgy.

He follows the same procedure for several more Sundays. Back, front, and next to her—always the same gesture of shaking her hand, displaying the "bait," and waiting for a response. But no response other than that smile.

He gets desperate. Now he croons songs during the Mass that ordinarily he would barely have sung. Parishioners don't know what to make of this crooner. But the choir director does. "Hey, why don't you join the choir? We could use you!"

"Why not?" Peter thinks. "More visibility. She's bound to notice." Oh yeah? She smiles as she always does but she doesn't rush up and gush over his singing.

So Peter decides he'd like to be an usher when he's not singing! That way he'd be able to escort her to her pew! "Ah! A brilliant idea," he thinks. So he escorts her not just to her pew but halfway into the pew! And yes, he gets exactly what he's always gotten from her—that smile. Nothing more.

By this time Peter is weary. He's tired of fishing for her attention. One evening as he's reading *Moby Dick* for the fourth time, he's thinking of everything he's done to get her attention—waiting at the church door, offering a sign of peace, posting his name and address on his lapel, singing in the choir, serving as an usher. He's convinced of only one thing. He's become a very active participant in the liturgies! But he's frustrated. He's tried everything—and gotten nowhere with the girl of his dreams. As he's thinking about this, he gets a phone call from his good friend, Grace Fisher. She tells him she has this terrific gal she'd like him to meet. Well, Peter's reaction is, "Forget it! I've had such lousy luck in the past couple of weeks. Why do I need more?"

"Oh, come on, Peter! You're trying too hard. You need a break!"

"OK," he sighs. Grace prevails!

The next night he goes to Grace's house, and guess who's there? Lo and behold, it's her! There he had plotted, ployed, postured, primped, and preened and nothing had come of it. Week after week! And now? Without any doing of his own, there he is face to face with her. And did they ever hit it off! Wow! WHAT A CATCH! All thanks to AMAZING GRACE!

Reflection

Like the apostle Peter, Peter in our story had been out in the boat doing everything possible to get a good catch—and got nothing! What does this tell us? You can be the best fisherman anywhere, casting your nets in the best waters, be in charge of the whole bait house, and have the biggest fishing fleet. But when it comes to getting a good catch, the catch that brings joy to your life—that makes it worth jumping out of bed in the morning and facing the day—well, no scheming, no angling, no contrivances, no plotting, ploying, primping, and preening, no charm, wit, or mint on the breath will do it!

Then what do we need to do to become somebody in another's eyes? That seems to be the question in this story. Peter tries everything he can to win the affections of the woman he meets at church. He succeeds in becoming very active in his church, but all his efforts to make the big catch are fruitless. She doesn't take the bait. Only after he's done all that he can to no avail does his friend Grace introduce him to the woman of his dreams.

It's a simple story about how to become somebody in another's eyes. We can't make it happen no matter what we do. We desire to be desired by someone we desire and either it happens or it doesn't.

Of course if we are as frenetic in our activity for God's approval as Peter was for the woman's, we'd really be in bad shape. Jesus' message was and is that we don't need to convince God we are worthy of being somebody in his eyes. It's a given.

The problem is if we've often been treated like a nobody by parents or friends or co-workers, we might feel God is no different. So we go overboard to prove ourselves to God. And the sad truth is there are very many whose experience is one of not having been loved by parents or siblings. So God's love is always a question mark for them.

Let's hope that we who believe God does accept us as we are might be a presence in others' lives who don't experience this love and be conduits in some mysterious way for Amazing Grace to make her appearance.

16. Remember!

Then the angel spoke, addressing the women: "Do not be frightened. I know you are looking for Jesus the crucified, but he is not here. Come and see the place where he was laid. Then go quickly and tell his disciples: 'He has been raised, from the dead and now goes ahead of you to Galilee, where you will see him.' That is the message I have for you." (Matthew 28:5–7)

Easter is one of those strange feasts when we fill Easter baskets with colored eggs on the one hand while we rejoice over Jesus' springing up to new life on the other. Seems as though Easter takes us in two different directions, doesn't it? I wonder if we can discover a connection between at least one famous egg and Jesus' new life—and how all of this helps us to celebrate the feast more fully. I have a hunch we might find that connection in something Jesus told his disciples the night before he was broken up and died on a cross. Before we get to what he said, however, we want to recall what happened to that famous egg who was also broken up and the mighty efforts others made to put him back together again.

Remember the nursery rhyme about that biggest of eggs, Humpty Dumpty? Remember, too, what happened to him? Many of us learned about him in a nursery rhyme.

16. Remember!

Humpty Dumpty sat on a wall
Humpty Dumpty had a great fall
All the king's horses and all the king's men
Couldn't put Humpty Dumpty together again!

Now why Humpty Dumpty was sitting on a wall is anybody's guess. Nothing like living dangerously! You know what it's like when you place an egg on a table and before you know it, it starts a slow roll toward the edge of the table and falls *plop* right on the floor!

Anyway Humpty Dumpty had a fall, a great fall! We don't know why he fell. Maybe he was snoozing in the noonday sun and simply rolled over. Or maybe he was prepping himself for an Easter egg role by recklessly rolling back and forth on the wall. The point is he fell on the hard pavement below and broke into a zillion pieces.

I think we can sympathize with Humpty Dumpty. We aren't eggs, but we break and shatter and hurt when something terrible happens. Somebody close to us dies. Or our doctor tells us we have serious health problems. Or we let someone down and we feel very bad about what we've done. Or folks in another country are suffering because they are being treated badly and this breaks us up. We can be so broken up that we die. I think that's what happened to Humpty Dumpty.

But when the king saw what happened, it didn't seem to bother him at all! He thought Humpty was a good egg, not hard-boiled inside—maybe a little too soft boiled, too caught up in others' problems. But the king wanted to bring him back to life. He got it into his head that if he used all the *power* he had, he could piece Humpty Dumpty together again and bring him back to life. I guess a lot of us think that power is supposed to solve every problem. "We need power to put Humpty back together again! Power! That'll do it!" the king cried as he marched out of his palace. He commanded all his powerful horses and soldiers to gather at the site where Humpty Dumpty had fallen off the wall.

First, he looked at his horses and, oh, what horses they were! Huge Clydesdales—the kind we see on TV around Christmastime hauling Ed McMahon in a wagon through the snow. The king smiled. "Talk about horsepower," he thought. "They'll do the trick!" So he ordered them to gather up all the eggshells that had been Humpty Dumpty and put them together. But guess what? Sure, their muscles were rippling and they were snorting like crazy, steam streaming from their nostrils like overworked locomotives. Yet powerful as they were, they had never noticed what Humpty looked like or what he had to say about himself when he was perched on the wall. They couldn't remember anything about him. So, they hadn't the slightest clue where all of Humpty's pieces belonged. The king was so disappointed he sent his powerful horses out to graze in the king's meadows until Christmas when once more they'd have to haul a heavier Ed McMahon through the snow!

Next the king ordered his most powerful soldiers to come before him. They got together in a huddle much in the same way a football team does during game time. Some of the soldiers looked like Arnold Schwarzenegger, square-jawed, bulging biceps, and even Austrian accents. Other soldiers looked like Jean-Claude Van Damme, and one bore a strong resemblance to Sylvester Stallone.

The king said, "Boys, now's the time to prove that all the money I've spent feeding you Burger Kings hasn't been in vain." Flashing razor-sharp teeth they growled, "No problem, boss!" Whew! Talk about confident! Grunting in unison they figured that since they had conquered huge armies in distant

lands, picking up old Humpty Dumpty's pieces and putting
him back together again would be a piece of cake!

But guess what? They grunted and groaned! They struggled
and strained! They huffed and puffed! Beads of perspiration
formed on their foreheads. Still they weren't about to give up!
Now they reversed their tactics! They groaned and grunted!
Strained and struggled! Puffed and huffed! But to no avail!
They wore themselves out trying to put ol' Humpty together
again but since they too had never bothered noticing what he
looked like or had to say about himself as he rolled daily
across the king's lawns, they couldn't remember where
Humpty's pieces belonged. The only egg they had was on their
faces as they slunk back to the king. The king was not pleased
and he ordered them to turn in their Vic Tanny Health Club
cards! Poor guys! Just when they thought they were in top
form!

Now what is it that all of the Clydesdales and all of the
Schwarzeneggers weren't doing that they should have been
doing? Why didn't the king's power get the job done? They
ought to have been present when Jesus told his disciples
what needed to be done when he was broken and dead so
they could share in his new life. Had they been there, then
Humpty Dumpty might be back sitting on the wall to this
very day. And what did Jesus tell his disciples? What did he
remind his disciples to do?

Certainly not to use force or power to get things done. This
didn't help all the king's horses and all the king's men put
Humpty Dumpty together again. Oh, sure, over the years people
in the church have used power to get things done—grunting and
groaning trying to force people to think this or that, trying to get
them to step in line with threats and nasty letters, and even
driving some out of the church. But that wasn't and isn't Jesus'
way.

16. Remember!

What, then, was his way? On the night before he died Jesus told his friends that if they wanted him to be present in their lives after he had been broken and died on the cross, they were to remember him in all that he said and did in what they said and did. Did you get that? Remember? That's it! That's how we are to experience him coming back together again in our midst. Remembering is the key to Jesus being alive and well with us? Yes, yes, yes!

It makes sense. Think of what we do when someone dies and we go to the wake. People who don't even know each other gather in groups of two or three and reminisce about their friend. They say, "Do you remember?" or "I recall" or "Remember when" and then they swap stories with one another about their friend—sad ones, goofy ones, loving ones. By the time the evening is over, everyone feels connected to everyone else because they have been remembering their friend's words and deeds and—miracle of miracles—in remembering they have been remembered with one another through their friend's spirit alive in their midst. Their friend's spirit lifts their spirits and may even inspire them to carry on some of the memorable things their friend did while he or she was alive.

Now when we remember Jesus' words and deeds as he tells us in the Mass, "Do this in memory of me," he too comes alive in us. We remember what he said and did and in saying and doing what he said and did, his spirit animates us to live as he did. Being compassionate or friendly or caring as he was is the way of experiencing his risen life in our lives.

"Remember." Such a beautiful word. We are the members of his body and we are re-membered—put together again as members of his Body—as we remember his words and deeds. Now we can do what all the Clydesdales and Schwarzeneggers couldn't do for poor, old, broken Humpty

Dumpty—we can remember our broken Jesus and, in remembering, experience his risen life in our midst.

Reflection

If lacking physical integrity meant being unclean in Jesus' day then the broken body of Jesus certainly signified his identification with the nobodies in his society. His crucifixion symbolized solidarity with those broken in spirit and body throughout his ministry. But Jesus broken and dying also symbolizes the life-giving power flowing from his being broken unto death.

Jesus tells us that the only way to avail ourselves of that life-giving power is by taking seriously what he said at the Last Supper, "Do this in memory of me." Do what? "Remember me!" How? In our breaking of the bread, we remember what he did whenever he broke bread during his ministry. He gathered the broken in mind, body, and spirit whom he claimed for the kingdom of nobodies through their table fellowship with him.

In our liturgies we remember by telling stories about what he said and did both at these meals and in the rest of his ministry. Remembering leads us to do in our own lives what he did. Saying and doing what he did we are remembered, experiencing ourselves as members of his Body.

If we forget, then we will be like those strong horses and strong men who got nowhere in their efforts to put Humpty Dumpty back together again. We will fall back on the abusive use of power.

Finally, to remember is both a gift to the one whom we remember and a gift from that person to us. By remembering the other we are giving thanks (Eucharist = thanksgiving) for

who and what the person has been for us. But the
remembered one brings us together and we are remembered
as Christ's Body through our remembering. Or to use Martin
Heidegger's words, " Thinking is thanking." But maybe Bob
Hope's words say it just as well, "Thanks for the memories!"

Lectionary References

Cycle A

Day of the Year	Story
4th Sunday of Advent	3. What's in a Name?
24th Sunday in Ordinary Time	13. Peter's Dilemma: How Many Times?

Cycle B

7th Sunday in Ordinary Time	11. The Crackpot
23rd Sunday in Ordinary Time	9. Absurd
30th Sunday in Ordinary Time	7. Turning a Blind Eye

Cycle C

5th Sunday in Ordinary Time	15. Going Fishing
14th Sunday in Ordinary Time	5. Mental Baggage
15th Sunday in Ordinary Time	4. Surprise!

Cycles ABC

Christmas (Mass at Midnight)	1. How Hark Became the Herald

Lectionary References

Bibliography

Crossan, John Dominic. *A Revolutionary Biography*. San Francisco: Harper, 1994.

Davies, Steven L. *Jesus the Healer*. New York: Continuum, 1995.

Malina, Bruce J., and Richard L. Rohrbaugh. *Social-Science Commentary on the Synoptic Gospels*. Minneapolis: Fortress Press, 1992.